WITH PAVLOV
ROUND THE WORLD

A HALT ON THE ROCKIES

WITH PAVLOVA ROUND THE WORLD

By
**THEODORE
STIER**

*Publishers
since 1812*

**HURST & BLACKETT, LTD.
PATERNOSTER HOUSE, E.C. 4**

First published c.1927

This facsimile edition published in 2019 by

The Noverre Press
Southwold House
Isington Road
Binsted
Hampshire
GU34 4PH

© 2019 The Noverre Press

ISBN 978-1-906830-85-4

ILLUSTRATIONS

WITH PAVLOVA ROUND THE WORLD

CHAPTER I

WHEN it is known that during the sixteen years I was her Musical Director I travelled with Pavlova no less than 800,000 miles, conducted 3,650 performances in which she took part, and over 2,000 rehearsals, it will be understood how close was our association.

It would serve no good purpose to enlarge here upon her genius. That would be stressing what already is universally acknowledged. My purpose is to enlighten those to whom her name is known as intimately as that of Duse, Coquelin, or Irving as to her diverse but infinitely fascinating personality, and to relate some of the curious and amusing incidents which from time to time occurred in our travels together. For, much as has been written of the dancer, but little has been placed on record of the private life of an artist whose energy is as amazing as her genius for friendship is remarkable.

As seems fitting for two such cosmopolitans, Pavlova and I met for the first time in London. At the time—1910—she was rather urgently in

need of a musical director for her forthcoming tour
in the United States, and upon the recommendation of my old friend and agent, Daniel Mayer,
she took the opportunity of judging my capabilities
for herself by attending the concluding concerts
which at the time I was conducting at the Bechstein
Hall—now the Wigmore Hall.

My first intimation of her interest was when I was
approached by Dan himself one day after Pavlova
had seen him and reported herself satisfied with my
performance.

" Do you speak French, Theodore ? " he enquired
anxiously.

I nodded.   " Yes," I said, " fluently, and other
languages besides."

Dan heaved a sigh of relief.

" Thank God ! " he said.   " Then you can go
and interview Madame Pavlova at her house at
Golders Green."

As may be imagined I lost little time in fulfilling
the appointment which he made for me there and
then.   When I arrived I found Pavlova sitting for
a ballet costume portrait to a famous artist for
a picture which to-day is known almost as well as
is the original.

At that interview I suspected what afterwards
I discovered to be one of her leading characteristics
—an acuteness of perception which renders her
correspondingly quick in coming to a decision.
In this instance our interview lasted not more than
five minutes before full terms were settled for my
engagement as her " Maestro."   From that time

forward, and except for the even more friendly
cher ami, she has addressed me by no other name.

As, a little on air perhaps, I recrossed Hampstead
Heath my thoughts travelled back to that not very
far distant day of my arrival in England from
Vienna. I was nineteen years old when upon a
morning which was as gloomy as my hopes were
bright I stepped from the boat at the port of
Grimsby, and armed with nothing more authentic
than those same aspirations, a firm determination
to succeed in this new land of my adoption, a
letter of introduction to a lady in Manchester, and
the sum of fourteen pounds ten in English money,
boarded the next train for Manchester. In spite
of these assets, however, I must admit that as the
train pulled out of the station, to match the day
perhaps, those high spirits had become considerably dampened, and that already I had begun to
feel terribly depressed, lonely, and homesick. From
my *Gazeteer* I see that Vienna is only some six or
seven hundred miles distant from my port of
landing. That first morning it seemed to me
more like six or seven thousand.

Nor, following my arrival, was my reception by
the younger, at least, of the inhabitants of Cotton-
opolis calculated to afford me the self-confidence
which is so necessary an asset for a first visit of
such importance as was the presentation of my
letter of introduction. It was close upon noon
before, having reached Manchester and booked a
room at some particularly modest hotel, I proceeded at once to change into the full evening dress

that on the Continent was the one correct costume in which at any hour a visit of formality might be paid, a garb which in my case was fittingly completed by the very opera hat which my father had worn at his wedding many years previously.

It will surprise none with any knowledge of the peculiarly forthright character of Lancashire folk to learn that I had not proceeded many yards towards my destination before I was leading the van of an ever-increasing army of small and very ribald boys, to whom the sight of a contemporary in full evening dress at high noon constituted a gratuitous entertainment from which it was obvious they intended to extract the last ounce of amusement.

Still heading the procession, however, I reached the beautiful house in Victoria Park at last. My faint and diffident ring at the bell was answered eventually by one of the most diminutive maid-servants I had ever seen, though I was to discover that her size was in inverse ratio to her appreciation of the ludicrous. At her first glimpse of me she broke into fits of prolonged and apparently uncontrollable laughter. However, I contrived at last to penetrate her amusement sufficiently to convince her that at least I had left my banjo at home; furthermore that I had good grounds for believing that her mistress would consent to see me.

Actually my hostess was kindness personified. So tactfully as to earn my everlasting gratitude she pointed out that here in England it was the custom to wear evening dress only at night. More

kind and practical still, she gave me a letter of
introduction to Willy Hess of the Halle Concerts,
who, receiving me with equal kindness, forwarded
me with a further letter of introduction to Glasgow.

My stay in the Scottish city was not of very
long duration, but even of that short hiatus in
my life there remains two unforgettable memories.
The first is of being, metaphorically at least,
hurled from my lodgings by a scandalised and Cal-
vinistic landlady for the unforgivable sin of playing
a Beethoven Sonata on the Sabbath ; the second
is of the insistence of Sir George Henschel, who
was my first conductor in Great Britain, that I
should wear warmer underclothing, and of his
kindness in taking me personally to the shop of
his recommendation to make sure, not only that
my purchases were of the correct kind, but that I
was not overcharged.

And now, after years of struggle so poignant
that sometimes I think it is a merciful dispensation
of Providence that with their passing so much of
their privation is effaced from my memory, I
found myself in a position as delightful as it was
unexpected. Nor in that walk across Hampstead
Heath was it altogether unpleasant to look back
upon an occasion earlier in my struggle when I
was entirely adrift, and thus glad to deputise for
a fee of 6s. 8d. in the very theatre for which ten
years later I was to be appointed Musical Director.

The thought brought others in its train of a
similar nature. I remembered an occasion only a
little later when with forty-one other aspiring

musicians I applied for one of the only two vacancies in the orchestra at Sir Henry J. Wood's second season at the Queen's Hall, an application in which most fortunately I was successful. With the knowledge of what since the Queen's Hall has become it was interesting to reflect that on the night of my first performance there was more than double the number of personnel in the orchestra than audience who had paid the price of admission. What the Queen's Hall is to-day is due, I am convinced, almost wholly to the sheer driving force and refusal to accept defeat of that fine fighting man and still finer musician, Sir Henry Wood. I am convinced further that London music as it is o-day owes more to him than to any other single enthusiast of late years.

However prolonged and bitter my own struggles had been, however, I was to find in Madame Pavlova a true comrade in the hard school of endeavour, for in no field of art or literature do I know anyone who had to fight more desperately for recognition than this truly great dancer.

The circumstances of our association were from the first so close as to lend themselves to an exchange of confidences.

For a considerable proportion of the time of that sixteen years her husband, and my own close friend, M. Dandré, either was in Russia or well in advance of the company, arranging forthcoming tours. At the beginning, particularly, though afterwards, as I shall show later, this came to be changed, practically the whole of her ballet were Russians who spoke nothing but their own language. Thus, as a fair linguist myself, I was called upon to act in the combined capacities of intelligence officer, liaison officer, billeting officer and interpreter for the whole company.

At such times, from eight o'clock in the morning until after supper each day, I was Pavlova's constant companion and cicerone. Simply it could not be helped ; that it should be so was necessary for our work. And in those few odd hours when the theatre did not claim either one or other of us it was natural that we should exchange personal reminiscences. And this is what, quite frankly and openly, she told me :

"My father died when I was two years old, and for all the remainder of my early life my mother's days and nights were spent in grim and unrelenting war against poverty. To whatever development I have been able to attain, then, I have much to thank my grandmother, who took me under her especial charge."

Her eighth birthday saw the turning point of her life, the guide-post that pointed so straightly towards the long steep road of artistry. On that day she was taken as a treat on her first visit to the theatre where was played the ballet of " The Sleeping Beauty."

It was a strangely silent little girl who trudged home that night through the snow-bound streets of St. Petersburg. It was as they were on the point of entering their small house that finally she could contain herself no longer.

" I know now, mother, what I am going to be,"
she burst out. " I am going to be a dancer."

That with Pavlova, the child was mother to the
woman is evident from the tenacity with which
in spite of all opposition she maintained her resolu-
tion. She gained her point at last, as so many
times since it has been gained, by sheer strength
of will.

That largely her talent is inborn is proved by
the fact that after trials which were as searching as
they were exhausting she was selected as a pupil
in that company of the elect who learnt at the
Imperial School of Dancing which at an annual
cost of two million roubles was maintained by
the late Tzar Nicholas himself. Once installed
there the regime was austere and rigid as that of
a nunnery, not only in the art for the fostering
and encouragement of which the institute was
founded, but in the completeness of its curriculum
of general education.

Discipline was severe in the extreme ; relaxation
entirely a secondary consideration to the main
purpose of the day. Only once a fortnight were
visitors permitted. Once a year the School was
honoured by a visit from its imperial but ill-fated
patron.

That, indeed, was a gala day, a day when each
pupil was keyed to the highest point to show what
they had learnt, instructors tense to justify their
work.

" I remember one visit of the Tzar," Pavlova
told me, " when there was one little girl with whom

he was particularly pleased, so that he picked her up and pressed a kiss on the top of her curly head. I remember, too, how bitterly I cried because I thought that it was I who should have been kissed instead of her."

When she was sixteen Pavlova passed out of the Imperial School to join the Corps de Ballet of the Opera House. Here, hard work was as continuous as had been the case at the School, though now so much of it was voluntary.

But hour by hour, day by day, Pavlova spent her time in practising. Dancing—always dancing —while other girls found time for pleasure.

It must be remembered that at this time Russia was the one country in which the art of the ballet owned a definite place in the field of artistic achievement. Thus, the name of a dancer might be a household word throughout the length and breadth of Russia and yet remain entirely an unknown quantity outside the borders of that country. This is why Pavlova came into her own with such supreme suddenness and as so great a revelation. For, long before her genius was recognised as universally as afterwards it came to be, she had won fame in St. Petersburg and Moscow.

And then one day a manager agreed to take her to Sweden, and in Stockholm it was that Pavlova reached the first milestone of an international career which in her own art has been one long progress from triumph to triumph.

At the close of her first performance there she was utterly and completely bewildered at the

behaviour of the audience. Even in her own
country she had not known the enthusiasm that
was displayed in Stockholm. When she came to
enter her carriage to return to her hotel she found
that the horses had been replaced in the shafts
by those whose tribute it was to drive her through
the streets. The carriage was followed the whole
way to the hotel by a crowd who roared their
applause of her.

"I could not understand it," she said to me.
"In Russia I did not think about myself at all.
Where there were so many of us it did not seem
possible that this thing could happen. Also I had
heard that though in Russia the ballet was taken
seriously, in other parts of Europe it was a dying
art that was only a graceful annexe, or complement,
to opera.

"So that you can judge of my state when the
next morning the manager of my hotel came to
me in great agitation to inform me that an equerry
from the Royal Palace desired the honour of an
interview. That gentleman told me that outside
there was a royal carriage to take me to the Palace
for the favour of audience with His Majesty the
King, so that he might pin upon my breast the
gold medal for Art and Sciences."

And that, as I have said, was Pavlova's first
triumph outside Russia, one which might so easily
have turned the brain of any young girl whose
head had not been placed very levelly and firmly
upon her shoulders.

It was, too, but the beginning. In Berlin, and

again in Paris, the enthusiasm for her performance was as tumultuous, almost, as had been the case in Sweden. It remained for London, the city which in outward regard is so philistine, but which once one has penetrated through to its inner heart is of all others the most appreciative and loyal, to provide the cold douche which for so young an artist was perhaps no very bad thing. In any case, having, as she considered, made no inconsiderable name for herself on the Continent, Pavlova came to London armed only with that reputation, a dictionary, and her own high courage.

She knew nothing of England, still less of those who would be likely to be of the best assistance to her career. I suppose it was inevitable that she should have chosen one of the lesser theatrical agents before whom to state her case. Here, then, is the dialogue which occurred when at long last she had sufficiently impressed her personality upon an impudent and not too physically clean office boy to induce him to bring her name before the proprietor.

Agent (*brusquely*). Well, Miss, what can I do for you ?

Pavlova. I am Madame Pavlova.

Agent. You don't say ! What is it you do ?

Pavlova (*patiently*). I am Anne Pavlova.

Agent. That means nothing in my young life. What do you *do*. Act, sing, or dance ?

Pavlova (*still more patiently*). I dance.

Agent (*brightly*). You dance, do you ? All right,

B

drop in to-morrow morning about eleven and bring your tights with you !

Poor London ! And yet though more than once when she has been asked which in her opinion are the world's three most beautiful cities, she has replied " Paris, Edinburgh, and Rio, but I should find it difficult to put them in their right order," her affection for London, as for all things English, and though of the heart rather than of the head, is as sincere as it is unmistakable. For does not the fact that never is she so happy as when at home in that beautiful Ivy House at Hampstead, which once was the home of the artist, J. M. W. Turner, prove that Pavlova no more can resist London than London can resist Pavlova ?

In any case, when some little time following her interview with that agent she appeared here, it was in full measure to repeat her Continental triumphs. At the express invitation of Lady Londesborough she made her debut in the town house of that great lady and hostess, and it was in the presence of King Edward and Queen Alexandra that a great artist and genius was launched. And so it was that in May of 1910 the girl who such a little time before had battered in vain at the door of a third-rate theatrical agent was secured by Mr. (now Sir Alfred) Butt for nine performances a week over a three months' season at the Palace Theatre, and following her first performance found herself described in the Press as one of the two greatest living artists then appearing on the stage.

PAVLOVA AND HER MOTHER IN THE GARDEN AT IVY HOUSE

Facing page 18

Speaking to me of that occasion some years later, Pavlova said :

" Life is a queer thing, and the whirligig of time more curious still. For just as I myself had waited in the cold for Duse to come out of the theatre in St. Petersburg, and implored her to touch me as she passed, so I remember a woman rushing out from that first night crowd and crying, ' I want you to touch my baby ! ' I do not remember ever having been so greatly moved as by the thought that by the gift of my art it should be within my power to affect people to an extent so overwhelming."

CHAPTER II

MY initial experience as musical director for Pavlova was on her first tour of the United States. It was at the first rehearsal at the Metropolitan Opera House in New York that occurred my introduction to that strange and wonderful body known as the Musicians' Union. And, being a first rehearsal, naturally I was over head and ears in work when the man approached me.

"Say," he said peremptorily, "I want to see you."

As the only thing in life that personally I wanted to see was my orchestra coming into line with my own ideas of how the music should be interpreted, perhaps I was a little curt in my reception of him.

"I'm sorry," I said, "but I can't see you or anybody else just now." And I raised my baton for the rehearsal to resume.

That baton, however, was destined not to fall, for without any further ceremony the stranger seized me by the arm.

"I guess you don't quite get me," he said dryly. "I'm the delegate of the Musicians' Union, and you just gotta talk to me whether you want to or not. Until you get my say-so you can't conduct this orchestra in Noo York or any place else on the

American continent, and you don't get that until you've complied with the regulations. You won't have complied with the regulations until you're a full-blown member of the Union. You can't be a member of the Union until you're an American citizen. So I guess you'd better can this here rehearsal and come along with me to see about it right now. Otherwise," he added warningly, " you're liable to find yourself in a jackpot."

All the time he had been speaking he had retained a tight grasp of my arm. I looked at him with an amazement which was caused as much by his colossal impertinence as by the suggestion of immediate nationalisation. With some knowledge of the unusually stringent regulations of the American Aliens Board I wondered how in the world he expected me to become a full-blown American citizen in the time between this rehearsal and our first performance.

I found that the explanation of the mystery lay in the extreme adaptability of American laws to the contingencies of the moment; that much which on the surface and to outward seeming is so full of sound and fury may be diluted to meet the need of that moment. It was so, in my case, with those harsh and autocratic Immigration Laws.

All that transpired—after, of course, I had paid the necessary subscription to the Union—was that some one placed a fiddle in my hand, I drew the bow across the strings in one chord and one chord only, and lo !—the ceremony was complete ! By the fulfilment of those mystic rites—of which I am inclined to think the former was by far the more necessary—I was entitled to conduct the orchestra and to take out what is known as my First Paper.

I was to find, indeed, that it was easier to obtain the consent of the Musicians' Union to conduct than actually it was to do so. At this stage of my career I thought that I had conducted under so many varied conditions that there was little in the art of which I had not expert knowledge. It was not until I came to conduct for Pavlova that I discovered one branch of my art at least in which I had quite a lot to learn.

In my innocence I had imagined, in conducting a ballet, that the dancer's feet followed the music according to my interpretation. I was wrong; utterly and completely. Strictly speaking the music does not control the dancing; actually the dancer leads, with the eyes of the conductor glued to her feet. As so many eminent musical directors have discovered to their chagrin, any method other than this results in a lack of synchronisation that is disastrous to the artist. Thus it will clearly be realised, also, how necessary it is for the conductor to have a knowledge of the music so complete as to be independent of the score. In point of fact I did not use a score for any work I conducted for Pavlova.

That first night at the Metropolitan Opera House on October 16th, 1910, was one of the great ordeals of my experience, one which was not helped by the ballet " Giselle," being the most difficult of all Pavlova's repertoire. In addition, the orchestra numbered no less than 107 performers, the control of whom was in itself something of a task. And even though I was able to thank the foresight which had led me to spend so many nights arranging my material, at the end of that first performance I was not surprised to discover myself drenched from head to foot in perspiration.

In many ways it was a curious life, this sixteen years of nomadism through the countries of the world. The Pavlova Company, indeed, was a little world of its own, with herself as benevolent but despotic queen, her husband, Victor Dandre, as Prime Minister, myself as—shall we say ?—Secretary of State for Domestic Affairs, and, whether her husband was with the company or away arranging for future tours, always that queen's devoted friend and confidant.

During those occasional absences of her husband, indeed, it was my custom as far as possible to relieve her of the extra work entailed. Each morning I would stand ready to take her to the theatre or shopping, lunch and dine with her, attend to her correspondence, and would not leave her until she retired for the night. It would not have been natural for an association so close to carry on from day to day without there being occasional cause for friction. To be frank, there were times when Pavlova was not as sunny as at others, for like all her sister and brother artists she is extremely sensitive, and, as later I shall show, inclined to be temperamental.

Our first misunderstanding arose only from that

kindly and impulsive generosity which is so much a part of her nature. We were in New Orleans at the time, and by accident I had discovered the imminence of her birthday. Without saying anything to her I communicated my discovery both to the company and to the orchestra, who seized the opportunity to subscribe to buy her a loving-cup to mark the occasion. Then it occurred to me that it might add value to our tribute if we took the audience into our confidence by making the presentation from the stage.

Everything passed off splendidly. Pavlova's surprise and delight were equally delightful to the audience, and when quite spontaneously she threw her arms round me and kissed me they nearly lifted the roof with their applause.

But that was only the beginning, for Pavlova is of the type whose first thought after receiving any little kindness is as to what pleasure she may give in return.

" What can we do for them, Maestro ? " she enquired anxiously, with a wave of her hand towards the company.

Eventually a picnic was decided upon. She hired twenty-five cars, and after rehearsal on a very hot Thursday afternoon she asked me to telephone the hotel at the appointed place to prepare a meal for everyone in the company, from herself down to the electrician and fireman.

Until immediately after tea the whole thing was a huge success. Everyone was happy and cheery, Pavlova most of all. Then it occurred to her that it would be a graceful tribute to " christen " the loving-cup which was the excuse for the picnic. She turned to me with one of her little imperious gestures.

" Where is the champagne, Maestro," she demanded. " I want champagne for the whole company."

Now though she had asked me to speak to the manager of the company on the matter of champagne, a rehearsal had prevented my doing so. In any case there was as much whisky and soda, beer, and light wines as to delight the heart of anyone not a fanatic on the subject of the Eighth Amendment.

" I'm sorry," I said, " but there was no time to arrange for it."

She looked at me with the expression of one whose whole world has been shattered to its foundations. From that moment the afternoon was irretrievably ruined, her party a dismal and abject failure. There and then she got into our car to take us home, and cried her heart out all the way back. As far, at least, as I was permitted to accompany her.

We travelled for some little distance in silence, a silence punctuated only by her sobbing. Then I could stand it no longer, and essayed a word of comfort.

" After all," I said consolingly, " who in the world wants to drink champagne at four o'clock in the afternoon ? "

She turned on me quickly, and in utter aversion.

"You say that just to absolve yourself from laziness," she cried, and leaning forward motioned the chauffeur to stop the car. "I beg you not to say another word," she added as he complied. And then, as the car slowed to a halt : "Please get out of my car immediately."

That was my first introduction to this particular mood, but I could see nevertheless that she meant exactly and precisely what she said. Get out of the car there and then I did, and hardly had my feet touched the ground before it was off again. Standing somewhat forlornly in the middle of the road I watched each succeeding car file past until the last of the procession, the one given over to the stage hands, drew alongside, and in that I made a not so luxurious but slightly less tempestuous journey to our hotel.

There was a sequel to the incident, however, which shows another and more lovable facet of her complex character. Except towards meanness or ill-nature Pavlova is incapable of nursing a grievance or of bearing malice. But though at this time I did not know her so well as afterwards became my privilege, I was more delighted than astonished when a couple of nights later, following a tap on the door of my dressing-room, I opened it to discover Pavlova with her arms outstretched.

She came at once into the room and threw her arms about my neck.

"Let us kiss and make friends, Maestro," she said. Than which no woman ever made more graceful or touching apology.

Equally childlike is her complete honesty of thought and expression. She is, I think, the most sincere woman it ever has been my good fortune to meet ; sincere with herself equally with others. There is no artist I know in any branch of life who takes greater pleasure in genuine appreciation. There is none I know with a more bitter detestation of empty compliments. And of these she has had a greater portion than most.

One perfectly dreadful manifestation of this is that in almost every town she visits she is pestered by the local dancing instructors to pass judgment on their work and pupils. That in no way is this in appreciation of or a tribute to Pavlova's genius no one knows better than herself. What those instructors are out for, of course, is something for nothing in the way of gratuitous advertisement.

Only rarely are they able to " get away with it," but there are times when even Pavlova may be overborne by sheer weight of importunity. Sometimes, taking the line of least resistance, she will consent to drop into the local dancing studio ; more rarely she will permit the instructor to bring a few selected pupils to the theatre after the performance to dance upon the stage. It used to be a source of secret satisfaction to me that these " gold diggers " had not the least idea of what they were letting themselves in for.

Their own healthy desire, of course, was for Pavlova to beam promiscuous approval on one and all, murmur a few words of praise which would reproduce well in the local newspapers and school prospectuses, and the proceedings be brought to an end to the satisfaction of everyone concerned.

What they omitted to take into account is that with Pavlova dancing is a religion. I have been the unwilling and embarrassed audience at more than one exhibition of dancing at which Pavlova has exercised her prerogative of high priestess. One such occasion, I remember, occurred in Denver, Colorado. Stark persistency on the part of the local terpsichorean expert induced Pavlova to consent to pass judgment on a few of the star pupils, who were to be shepherded to the theatre for the purpose. I watched her face as the bedecked children went through their gyrations, and from my knowledge of her realised that there was trouble brewing. The music ended, the dancers' feet at long last stilled, the staff stood waiting to receive the congratulations they were so sure were merited by the performance.

Pavlova, who had been watching from the footlights, stood up, her face white with anger. She spoke slowly and very distinctly.

" Here there is no talent, and a method which is wholly wrong," she said. " Where is the teacher ? Let me speak to her."

To a tone so incisive there could be but one reply. The cowering instructress came forward to the footlights.

" I consider it utterly disgraceful that you ever should have presumed to teach dancing," Pavlova said icily, and when Pavlova is icy the Arctic regions are warm and sunny by comparison.

" Not only are you incompetence personified," she went on in the same tone, " but you are spoiling years of these children's lives. And now," she added, " will someone please conduct me to my car."

But that instance is but another facet of a character which is wholly complex but wholly lovable. When she praises, appreciation comes from the heart ; when she condemns it is entirely without compromise. Take, for example, her invariable reply when asked her opinion of jazz music.

" To me it is the very lowest form of amusement, and one for which I have nothing but the most supreme contempt. It is entirely without beauty ; the music a horrible noise made by instruments that are raucous in the extreme, and which emit only an intensified form of savage rhythm. Furthermore, so far as concerns the dancing, there is in it a pretence of harmlessness which in reality contains an underlying viciousness that is calculated to cause an infinity of harm."

But more dominant even than her quickness of temper or uncompromising honesty of thought and word is an undeviating, untiring, driving-force which has the power to communicate itself to every member of her company. If it fails to do so in any individual case that person's association with her is not likely to be of long duration. It is this fervour which even more than her genius is responsible for the position she occupies to-day. She is, indeed, the most ardent disciple of the theory that genius is one per cent inspiration and ninety-nine per cent perspiration I have met.

It does not matter how long or tiring the railway or car journey may have been, it is rare for her to go to her hotel in a town where she is booked to appear before she has first visited the theatre. There, in all probability drenched in perspiration where the ordinary actor would shiver desperately with the cold, one may find her practising in some corner of a dark and desolate stage hours after the rest of the company are safely housed and fed.

Thus it is not surprising that she exacts from her company the same undeviating devotion to their work as she gives to her own. So far as her art is concerned, indeed, she is the complete autocrat, a quality of which in ordinary intercourse she gives but little indication. I have said many times to new-comers in the company that the sooner they realise how clearly defined is the line of demarcation between Pavlova the woman and Pavlova the artist the more readily they will settle down, and the sooner their performance will reach that smooth perfection short of which Pavlova never will be satisfied. At the beginning, the difference between the cheery tender-hearted woman whose wide sympathy goes out so spontaneously to every sort and kind of suffering, and the relentless taskmaster on the stage, was absolutely staggering. It was quite a few days before I realised that the moment Pavlova entered the stage door she forgot friends and ties and everything in life but her own burning enthusiasm for the art in which her whole existence is bound.

It cannot be denied that there are times when this white light of enthusiasm leads her to demand from others what but for her own driving force would be impossible. Quite frequently I have known her insist that an orchestra of twenty should sound like a band of fifty performers.

Without a word of explanation or apology I have known her to take the arrangement of the ballet out of the hands of the ballet master himself, and, completely ignoring his presence, arrange it to suit her own artistic conception of the theme. Climatic conditions she ignores; heat or cold or damp affect her not at all. Lack of rest on the part of her company or staff makes no appeal to her that is not overborne by her demand for perfection. What she herself can do, others can and are made to accomplish.

Yet once she is outside the theatre all this autocracy leaves her as a garment; in that transition she becomes once more the most kindly, the most sincere, and the most democratic of friends—understanding, sympathetic, and of a generosity unbelievable.

The full extent of her private charities, indeed, is known to none but herself. Actually, I doubt very much if even she has any very exact realisation of their extent. But though she gives almost universally, there is one charity in particular to which she devotes herself with an enthusiasm which is as practical as it is far-reaching. This charity, which she founded in 1920 at a personal cost of 320,000 francs, is her Orphan Home in the Rue Chemin de Fer at Paris.

Here, twenty refugee children from the holocaust which once was Russia are educated, fed, clothed, and cared for, and when at last they pass out into the world which but for her would be so cold and desolate a place, it is to an occupation which is fitting to their talents and disposition. If Pavlova had done no other good in her life, that Home would yet remain the permanent memorial of a gallant and great-hearted woman.

Outside her work this is her great hobby and preoccupation. Constantly her thoughts turn to how best she may serve it. On her birthdays, for instance, it has become her custom to request her company to send to this Home the money which otherwise they would have subscribed towards a present for herself. Whenever her other engagements permit, it is her delight to give a special charity performance, the whole proceeds of which go to the institution which is so near her heart, and with each occupant of which she has kept in close and constant touch since the day of its foundation.

Again, she is intensely and fervently patriotic. To her, Russia is a shrine of mingled tenderness and grief to which every day her thoughts yield sacrifice. In outward seeming the most cosmopolitan of women, at heart she is a Russian of the Russians, of purely Russian temperament and habit of mind. Apart from the upkeep of her Home there is nothing which affords her so keen a delight as to send help and succour to any of her old friends of the Petrograd Opera House who, having escaped the cockpit of the revolution, are yet in need of assistance.

In common with all great-hearted people, of course, she is continually being imposed upon and swindled. To many, her experiences in this direction would have brought disillusion and complete loss of trust in the fundamental goodness of human nature ; Pavlova they have left unscathed. She does not know what the word cynicism means, and while very far indeed from being a fool, the inborn desire to help others, which is one of her strongest impulses, continues, and will always so continue, to render her an easy prey to the cheat and the hypocrite.

It is not so much that she gives indiscriminately ; actually she makes a show of investigating each case which is submitted to her. Her weakness is that always her inclinations are so much towards the under dog that the benefit of whatever doubt there may be is diverted in favour of the supplicant. " Better thrice to be imposed upon than once to turn the empty away " is the motto upon which her charity is founded.

I remember an occasion in Madrid when she came to me in tears and thrust a letter into my hand.

" Read it," she said brokenly. " Isn't it pitiful. And how right that she should come to me, a sister artiste."

o

I read the letter. Apparently it was a last-minute appeal from a Frenchwoman who wrote that while once, like Pavlova, she had been a famous and successful dancer, now, poverty-stricken and broken in health, she was lying penniless and bedridden in a local garret.

It was a moving epistle. Too moving, to my idea; the agony was piled on a little too profusely to carry entire conviction. When I gave this as my opinion, and urged Pavlova to caution, she was indignant. I was hard-hearted and callous, lacking in understanding and the true warmth of human sympathy. No one I know can be more eloquent and in a greater variety of languages than Pavlova when she is moved.

" On the contrary," she said firmly, " I am going to ask you to take her a hundred pounds at once."

Frankly, I was not sorry that the mission had been entrusted to me. A hundred pounds is a hundred pounds, and there was something about that begging letter which aroused in me a determination to see the thing through to the finish.

When I reached the address, however, I wondered for the moment if my caution had not outrun my sympathy. On the face of it everything was entirely as the writer had painted it. In that sordid garret lay a lady, still young and with the ravaged remains of considerable beauty, but bedridden and quite obviously in a serious condition. Her story, related in more detail than had been practicable in a letter, carried a certain verisimilitude.

But as she told it I watched her closely, and the longer she spoke the more convinced I became that she was not as she represented herself. To use a colloquialism, I have covered a bit of ground in my time, and to my sorrow I had seen that particular type of illness before, an illness the symptoms of which once perceived by the initiated, never afterwards can be mistaken.

My cross-examination was, I trust, kindly; in any case it was very thorough. Eventually she broke down and owned up. Her illness was due entirely to drugs.

Whether that terrible habit was cause or effect of her condition was not my function to enquire. My instructions from Pavlova were specific; to relieve the supplicant's immediate necessities. And the girl—for she was little more—was ill, terribly in debt, and liable at any moment to be turned out of her lodgings.

Nevertheless I did not give her the hundred pounds which Pavlova had thrust upon me for the purpose. Instead I reduced the gift by seventy-five per cent, and having consoled her with the not unsubstantial benefaction of twenty-five pounds, said good-bye with the consolatory feeling that I had seen the last of a particularly unpleasant job. In which, however, and as events transpired, I was unduly optimistic.

From Madrid the company went on to Paris, and we had not been there very long before a second letter arrived from Madrid in which Pavlova was implored to send the unfortunate woman back to Paris, where, under the influence of her little son, she might find reclamation. By all the gods she knew she vowed that once in her native city she would give up the dope habit and do all in her power to rehabilitate herself in her profession.

That great writer, O. Henry, begins one of his stories : " No doubt you have been touched with, and by, actors ! " In this case Pavlova was touched both ways, in heart and pocket, and upon her instructions I purchased the necessary ticket from Cook's and forwarded it to Madrid.

I was neither surprised nor disappointed when a reasonable time elapsed with no acknowledgment forthcoming. I waited another week or ten days, however, and then called upon Cook's, reminded them of my purchase, and asked them to enquire if the ticket had been used. A day or two later I called again and found that it *had* been used— but not in the way it was intended. Actually it had been returned to their Madrid office, and upon the woman's instructions, and less, of course, the usual ten per cent agent's commission, the money paid for it refunded to her. Further investigation proved her to be a professional begging-letter writer, whose system it was to attempt this same ticket trick upon practically every famous artist who visited the Spanish capital.

Pavlova was sorry, of course, but accepted the swindle with her usual large-hearted tolerance. Her view is that it is so easy to forgive people who must find it so hard to forgive themselves.

There is a greatness in Pavlova's charity which

the mere giving of money is wholly inadequate to satisfy. "It is no sacrifice," she says, "for the rich to part with what they cannot miss." So that it is her delight to render in personal service what cannot be reduced to terms of money.

An instance of this occurred in a small town in the United States. There was one member of her company whose habit it was on arriving for the first time at any fresh theatre to make a wild dash to secure the most comfortable dressing-room to which her position in the company entitled her.

She had been warned more than once of the risk she ran in doing this without having first ascertained the geography of the building. Small-town theatre proprietors are not noted for a hypersensitive regard for the convenience or safety of those who perform in the buildings they control. Security costs money, and the less cash they pay out in structural efficiency the bigger the annual profit. Hence it is not surprising that in dashing through a strange and ill-lighted theatre the girl should have fallen through a trap-door down the height of two full stories.

Pavlova's distress was immeasurable, and, moreover, at once took practical form. After she had recovered from the shock of the news her first action was to turn over her own drawing-room for the sole use of the patient. From that moment she devoted to the stricken girl all the hours of each day and night until the pain had abated sufficiently to allow of the patient being left for a little while. It was only then that in an interview

with the doctor the latter broke it to Pavlova that
the patient never would be able to dance again.

To Pavlova, of course, that was the most profound misfortune of all possible misfortunes, equivalent to a living death. Again her sympathy took
practical form, this time by the inauguration of a
subscription list which her own name headed with
an amount only she would have thought it necessary
to subscribe. Before she left the company the girl
was handed a cheque sufficient to keep her in
comfort and medical attention for some very
considerable time.

Nor was this the end. Pavlova never forgets
a friend or a member of her company. It was
two years later that, included among her letters
one morning was one which contained a cheque
she had contributed towards the building of a
new wing of a certain hospital, but the work
having been found impossible to accomplish, the
subscriptions were returned to the various donors.
This was unexpected money, of course, and immediately Pavlova's mind turned to speculation as to
the good she might do with it. She sat in silence
for a few moments. Suddenly her face brightened,
and with one of her little quick gestures she handed
the cheque to me.

" Let us find that poor girl L——," she said,
" and give her this."

It was a long and difficult search, but eventually
we ran our quarry to earth in a meagre room on
the fourth floor of a poor house in a still poorer
district of New York.

The girl was still an invalid, and had very few friends; I think, indeed, it was the forlornness of her condition even more than her physical disability that was preying so desperately on her spirits.

Pavlova's visit came to her as running water in a parched and arid land. Never shall I forget the look which transfigured the girl's face as we entered the room, nor of the wonder in her eyes when she saw the cheque. But starkly needful as the money was, it was the knowledge that the gift was inspired by a two years' remembrance which was still green and fragrant that sublimated and rendered it a thing of so much the greater joy.

That loyalty, however, was only on all fours with Pavlova's care for the girls of her company. In trouble or sickness, as in their work or pleasure, there is not one but is assured of her sympathy and understanding. It is her pride to stand in the light of mother and guardian to " her girls." She makes it her personal consideration to interest herself in the food they eat, the clothes they wear, and, more urgently still, of the reputation of the hotels in which they stay.

In this matter of the girls' moral well-being Pavlova feels the strongest personal responsibility. At the beginning of my association with her the company was almost exclusively Russian, and hence censorship in that direction was far more difficult than it grew to be afterwards. They were a pretty trying lot, some of those Russians.

They used to drive Pavlova nearly frantic sometimes. Brilliant they may have been, quite a lot of them, but they had only the smallest notion of playing the game. The company was split up into cliques and factions, each warring relentlessly against the other, and for no two weeks running was the personnel of these contending bodies the same, so that it was a matter of the most delicate diplomacy to maintain a stable equilibrium between any two of them—desertions were so many and frequent. Jealousies were rampant, of course; it was impossible for Pavlova to take friendly notice of one without bringing the wrath of practically the whole of the rest of the company on her head.

I think if this temperamentalism had been caused by anything like her own devotion to their art she would so much more readily have forgiven them.

But it was nothing of the kind; they drove her almost to distraction by their unpunctuality both at rehearsals and for the actual performance. Their continual demands for leave of absence for their own pleasure was equally galling to one whose passion for her art amounts almost to a religion.

Eventually, as an experiment, a small leaven of English girls was introduced into the company, and with such success that gradually as the Russian girls left they were replaced wholly from England and Scotland until the whole ballet was British.

Then began an era of peace for Pavlova such as she had not thought it possible to exist. The girls quickly learnt their job, they were keen and loyal, friendly towards each other, and of a cheerfulness

under difficulties which after the wails and lamenta-
tion of the Russians was a revelation.

It was now that Pavlova accepted responsibility
for the moral well-being of her girls. It must be
remembered that the ballet was recruited mostly
from English girls of good family and education,
the mothers of whom at first were a little dubious
about entrusting their daughters to the care of
a stranger of whose personal character they knew
little, and for a tour which would take them into
many strange lands and into contact with so many
strange peoples. It was the talks she had with
these English mothers which impressed her with
the nature of the trust she had undertaken. I
should like to say here that in not one of our tours
after the advent of the British recruits would it
have been possible to find a cleaner, more cheery
or devoted company than that which Pavlova
succeeded in gathering to her banner. I am never
able to think of these girls without a feeling of
admiration for their courage under new and, quite
frequently, extremely hard conditions, for their
unremitting cheerfulness under the fatigue of hard
work and incessant travelling, and their loyalty,
not only to Pavlova and their ballet master and
musical director, but what is of even greater
moment, their loyalty to themselves and their own
self-respect.

In this spirit of mutual goodwill Pavlova's
co-operation was as frank and appreciative as it
was sincere. Just so long as it was apparent that
a girl was acting up to the spirit of her implied

contract she never once made the mistake of undue interference. On the other hand, however, on the rare occasions when she had just cause for complaint, retribution was as swift as it was decisive. Thus, when one of those curious creatures, an American hotel detective, discovered one of the lady members of the company in what it must be admitted was a singularly compromising situation, and without hesitation turned her into the street in the early hours of the morning, Pavlova's reaction to the reflection cast upon the company was immediate.

At nine o'clock that same morning the delinquent was summoned to the sitting-room of her suite.

"Here is your salary to date, with a fortnight in advance, and a railway ticket and reservation to New York," Pavlova said icily. "There you will be met by my agent and taken to an hotel in which rooms will already have been reserved for you. There you will remain until the sailing of the next available boat for England, upon which he will see you to your berth. Good morning."

But when a girl left the company in the ordinary way she did not say good-bye without carrying with her a memento of her association with the great Pavlova, and more often than not the farewell gift was one of considerable value. In particular I remember one girl who after some years with the company left us to be married. At the little celebration dinner that was given as her God-speed, Pavlova presented her with a horseshoe brooch set with the same number of very beautiful diamonds as the years of their association—eleven.

At the end of my own first season with her I was the recipient of a memento in the shape of a diamond tie-pin. I have always lamented the ill-luck which ordained that of the presents I have received from her from time to time it was this particular one that was stolen.

Pavlova has a passionate desire that every girl who comes under her charge shall turn into a dancer of distinction. That after showing real promise one should leave the company was a matter of real grief to her. This is instanced in the case of a Scottish girl who appeared likely to become an outstanding success. In her enthusiasm Pavlova gave up many afternoons of rest to the hard work of perfecting her talent. It must be admitted that in an anxiety to develop her pupil's ability she was perhaps a little chary in praise.

Calling in at Pavlova's dressing-room one night I found her in tears.

For a long time she refused to give me any explanation of her trouble. I coaxed and pleaded all I knew, and eventually it all came out.

" M—— has left me," she cried between her sobs. " Actually she has decided to give up ballet dancing for "—the contempt in her voice was unimaginable—" *musical comedy!* " Then, tragically, and after a pause : " Musical comedy ! . . . I was too proud to argue with her—I just had to let her go. But she will ruin her chances for all time."

Again, her head on her arms, she gave way to tears. For a long time there was nothing I could say which had power to console her. To her the defection of that Scottish girl was the cause of greater unhappiness than one could have imagined possible.

There were in that rather pathetic little interview two elements which, because they were so mutually contradictory, were also typical of her character.

She was too proud to argue with a girl whose defection cut her to the quick; she was not too proud to give way to her grief in front of me.

CHAPTER III

LIKE so many great artistes, Pavlova is subject to her temperament. Her moods alternate like the English weather in April, and she is almost completely at their mercy.

Perhaps it is the little things which affect her most, and from her descend in happiness or depression throughout the whole company. The presence or the lack of a little sunshine either of mood or in nature is inclined to alter the whole tempo of her work throughout the day.

The company of a person whom particularly she may like or dislike is one of the chief causes of a sudden change of mood. A letter, or the non-arrival of one she has been expecting, affects her with equal force. Thus it is necessary for all concerned, and particularly for Pavlova herself, that immediately she enters the theatre it should be ascertained if all is well with her, and to discover which of her various moods is uppermost. This is all the more essential on account of the real physical risk entailed by her work, and the manner in which that work is affected by her mood. A pirouette taken either too quickly or too slowly might at any time entail disaster.

Even when the performance is at an end there are times when it is extremely difficult to induce her to leave the stage; indeed, if she is really dissatisfied with her own performance, nothing will persuade her to go to her dressing-room until the fault is rectified. Oblivious of everything in earth or heaven, she will stay on practising until the audience has left and the theatre plunged in darkness. No sacrifice of time or energy is too great a cost for that ultimate finish which is so individual to herself.

The strain involved in her work, and the corresponding drain upon her vitality, renders it essential that her recreations shall be soothing to her nerves and physical strength. One of her favourite relaxations is to drive slowly through the country, assimilating, in all their beauty, the colours of field and hedgerow, flowers and fleecy clouds, for she is amazingly sensitive to colour and form. Surprisingly, for one of her temperament, she has no very great love for books. Instead of reading she prefers to visit museums and picture galleries, or to wander in old places of worship.

But the greatest of all her pleasures, and one in which she becomes so absorbed as to forget even her dancing, is her hobby of modelling in clay. I write hobby, but it is far more than that. Indeed I venture the statement that in gaining its greatest dancer the world has lost a sculptress of only little lesser comparative genius.

This matter of artistic self-expression was inspired originally by her friend, Malvine Hoffman, the sculptress who is responsible for the group on the northern side of Bush House. But though

FROM ONE ART TO ANOTHER—PAVLOVA MODELLING IN CLAY

Facing page 46

entirely self-taught, there are groups of classical dancers from Pavlova's chisel which in grace and vitality bear comparison with the work of many of the better known sculptors.

Cards, Pavlova regards entirely in the spirit of fun ; she has not the temperament of the gambler. The game of poker she enters into with a naive zest to which the winning of a few shillings brings an almost childish delight. I have known her dance around the room for five minutes on end because the game has left her half a crown to the good ; a dance for which her professional fee would have been something like a couple of hundred pounds.

Of all the petty annoyances of her daily life the importunate stranger is her pet aversion. This is a pest from which all prominent people suffer, but Pavlova more than most, and it is a constant source of rather pained wonder to her how ready a certain type of individual is to sacrifice all personal dignity in the endeavour to make her acquaintance. And her method of dealing with these people is as peremptory as in ninety-nine cases out of a hundred it is effective.

I remember an instance which occurred during a brief summer holiday in Monte Catini which illustrates her methods to a nicety. During the whole of the daylight hours she had been tracked by two ladies with the untiring persistency of hunters stalking big game, and had succeeded only in infuriating Pavlova during the process.

" Thank goodness," she said as we returned to the

hotel for dinner, " we have seen the last of those insufferable women."

Unfortunately for the two lion hunters, however, Pavlova's self-congratulation proved premature, for when that same night we visited the opera she discovered that the very next box to our own was occupied by her two *bêtes noires* of the morning and afternoon. " I shall stay in the box," Pavlova said firmly, " for the sole purpose of avoiding them."

But even in that precaution she underrated the persistency of these two very determined ladies. For with the interval when the lights went up and we were chatting happily together came a loud knock on the door, and without waiting for a reply the handle turned, and to my astonishment and Pavlova's fury both women swept smilingly into the box. " We are real sorry to intrude," the self-elected spokesman exclaimed, " but we felt we couldn't go home without taking the opportunity of shaking hands with the world-famed Madame Pavlova."

As Pavlova got up from her seat the look with which she favoured her visitors was such that it seemed to freeze her countenance to an icy mask of contempt, and the faces of the two ladies to blank and abject consternation.

" My name is Madame Dandré," she said. " Of the lady of whom you speak I have no knowledge whatever, nor do I desire the honour of your acquaintance. Will you be so good as to leave my box."

Another example of a somewhat similar nature occurred when it came to her ears that, without in any way approaching her, a certain social climber in the neighbourhood of Grosvenor Square had announced to all and sundry that Pavlova was to dance at a forthcoming house party. In common with other incidents I shall have to relate, it has been attributed in current gossip to more than one person of contemporary prominence. In each case, however, it is within my personal knowledge that the episode happened, actually, to Pavlova.

Already more than a little annoyed by the liberty taken with her name, Pavlova was at her most dignified when eventually she was approached as to the amount of her fee.

" Five hundred pounds," she said.

To which, looking rather staggered, the newly-rich lady enquired what programme Pavlova intended to submit in the event of their coming to terms, in each case enquiring the time which the particular item under discussion would occupy—queries of which for some time Pavlova was unable to realise the drift. Then, with a sudden reversion to type, the hostess provided illumination.

" Surely five hundred pounds is a very great deal of money for a performance which will last only five or six minutes ? " she protested.

Pavlova hates nothing so much as barter. In this case, however, she was calmly and contemptuously firm.

The prospective hostess was more than firm ;

D

she was definitely rude, an element which left Pavlova unmoved. Eventually the newly enriched lady was forced to give way.

" As I have given it out to my guests that you are to appear," she said with a shrug of her massive shoulders, "what else can I do but submit to terms for which I can find no other expression than exorbitant."

In one quick glance Pavlova appraised the elaborate and unduly ornate appearance of the room in which the interview took place ; took in also her still more ornate and elaborately caparisoned hostess, and in doing so was able to visualise the type of audience before whom she would be called upon to dance.

" If you do not insist upon my sitting with your friends at supper," she suggested generously, " I will reduce my fee to three hundred pounds."

Those who do not know her well may be inclined to regard this sensitiveness as undue arrogance. if that is so the impression is ill-founded. Once her outer reserve is penetrated there is no more simple or less affected woman living. Partly this isolation of manner is due to natural shyness ; partly—particularly was this the case upon her first arrival in England—it may be caused by ignorance of the language. Illustrative of this last was her expression of delight and appreciation when not long after her arrival in London from a foreign tour she received an invitation couched in the familiar formula : " The Duke of Manchester requests the pleasure of Madame Pavlova's company. . . ."

She handed the card to me, and as I took it, clapped her hands excitedly.

"Knowing that I myself do not go out, how very kind of him to ask my whole company!" she exclaimed.

It is a tribute to her innate good breeding, however, that the more eminent the society in which she finds herself, the less diffident her manner becomes. In the presence of Royalty, and of British Royalty in particular, she is ease and naturalness personified. As I have told already, the occasion of her first appearance in England was at the house of Lady Londesborough, and in the presence of the late King Edward and Queen Alexandra.

Later, during a four weeks' season at the Queen's Hall, her late Majesty again was present, and actually presented Pavlova with the bouquet which she herself had accepted from the management. In the course of the conversation which followed the Queen requested Pavlova to send her a signed photograph.

It was a matter of sincere regret to Pavlova that in the rush of her daily life she forgot to fulfil her promise, an omission of which, however, she was reminded later by Queen Alexandra herself. It was two years afterwards when for the second time the great dancer was honoured with a command to present herself in the Royal box.

"Really I should be very angry with you," the

Queen said with a gracious smile which entirely negatived the rebuke. "Long ago you promised to send me your photograph. I do so hope that now you will permit me to have it."

In speaking of Pavlova's shyness it must not be thought that she allows it to come between herself and her own natural kindness of heart. Many times I have known her go out of her way to be companionable with strangers when her own inclinations were towards nothing so much as supper and bed. Once, in Edinburgh, an elderly Scotsman and his wife, who were staying at the same hotel as ourselves, took what doubtless they considered the diplomatic step of first making acquaintance with myself; a move, had they known it, with which I was only too familiar. However, the acquaintance once upon what they thought sufficiently firm ground, they begged me to persuade Pavlova to accept their hospitality for supper one night after the performance.

As firmly as might be I replied that Pavlova made it a rule to make no new acquaintances. Her objection, I explained, was due not to discourtesy, but only to the absolute necessity for nursing a vitality upon which her art made such strenuous demands. This rule was so strict that never under any circumstances could she be persuaded to depart from it.

I found, however, that Pavlova's persistency in refusing hospitality was matched equally by that with which the old Scotsman pleaded that at least I should give Pavlova a chance to decline this particular invitation. Finally, as the line of least resistance, I gave way.

Having capitulated, moreover, I felt that it was up to me to play the game in the spirit as well as merely to the letter. Consequently I waited until I was able to catch Pavlova in what I know to be a favourable mood. Then, with a cajolery equal to that of the Scotsman himself I succeeded in wringing from her a reluctant consent to accept the proffered hospitality.

Armed with the glad tidings I hurried across the corridor to the old couple, who were beside themselves with happiness at the news. A night was agreed upon, and all arrangements made.

But when the time came, alas! Pavlova was renegade. The day had gone hardly with her, and the quickly alternating springs of her vitality were at their lowest ebb. Reluctantly, but not without good reason, she decided that she was too tired to keep the appointment.

When I reached the room of that kindly Scottish couple for the purpose of breaking the news, I found it made lovely with innumerable flowers, and that already the table was laid for supper. I have had many more pleasant tasks in my life than the one I was charged with then.

The old lady, in particular, seemed cut to the heart, and when I told her that Pavlova was in bed and probably asleep, her distress was such that I do not want to witness anything like it again. There was only one thing to do—hurry back to Pavlova and tell her that, dying or dead, she must get up and come to that party.

Not unreasonably, one of her first questions was to ask me why, in this particular instance, I had gone over to the enemy. When I told her the circumstances, and made her realise that she had been the cause of real pain to an old couple whose only desire was to give her pleasure, my point was gained. Without troubling to add more than a very loose and informal négligée to her night attire, she hurried at once across the corridor and burst impetuously into the old couple's room, all sense of shyness lost in an urge to mitigate their disappointment.

Five minutes later that trio were like three birds on a bough, chattering volubly in French as if they had been close friends for years.

As a result of what turned out to be a very cheery and interesting evening, two parcels were delivered into the respective rooms of Pavlova and myself the following morning. Pavlova's gift was a Scottish claymore, the hilt of which was studded with jewels. My own memento as intermediary was the characteristically Scottish present of a gold purse.

One rather amusing eccentricity of Pavlova's is that while she seems always to be buying clothes, she appears never to have time to wear them, so that eventually the very large majority are destined to find their way into the wardrobes of the company. But where she is thus indifferent to frocks, she has a perfect passion for every description of footwear. Her dancing shoes have been made by the same firm in Milan for many years, and thus she has not to trouble her head about them. It is footwear for ordinary occasions over which she spends such an extraordinary amount of time and care.

It is a grim day for the company when the word is passed round that Pavlova is going to buy shoes. To me its harbinger was the inevitable approach of M. Dandré with the request that I should take her out " shopping." For some months I was deceived by the frank ingenuousness of his approach, for he is nothing if not a diplomatist. Later, however, I " got wise," as the Americans say.

" My dear friend," I would exclaim hurriedly, " I should be absolutely delighted, but the fact is I have a rehearsal that'll take me practically the whole day. I'm afraid you can't count on me. What about yourself ? "

Dandré would throw up his hands.

" Nothing I should like better," he would protest, " but as you know, my appointments forbid."

" Then there is no one for it but——" and I would mention the name of the ballet master. Sometimes I won, at others I was beaten, in which case I knew that I was doomed to long hours in a boot shop, what time Pavlova turned over shoes in endless variety of shape and pattern. It is to be said for her that I have never known her come out of a shop without making a purchase ; equally I have never known her really satisfied with any pair of shoes that ever she has bought.

With people with whom she is familiar her conversation is animated and of considerable depth of thought and observation. Like so many of her compatriots her favourite themes are art, politics, and religion, for she is deeply and sincerely religious. Each great festival of the Orthodox Russian Church she keeps with rigid fidelity.

One need be in her company for only a very little time to be able to realise her for one of those rare spirits whose belief in the gospel of equality and fraternity is no mere lip service, but that in the spirit and essence of that great creed she lives and has her being. And although she is a sufferer from the present chaos that once was Russia to the extent that her old home is closed to her for ever, she loves her native country with a whole-hearted passion which longs only for its future greatness and well-being.

Much of Pavlova's charm in everyday life is due to her unusually keen sense of humour. I remember once in Carecas, the capital of Venezuela, when the then President, General Gomez, presented her with a red velvet jewel case upon the raised top of which her name was emblazoned in gold pieces of the denomination of twenty-five dollars each, how for a moment she regarded the ornate gift with an expression of awe that only half succeeded in concealing her amusement.

However, it was with her usual charming smile that she expressed her thanks to the distinguished donor. Then, after a pause, she added whimsically :

" This is the first time in my life that I regret

my name is Anna Pavlova." Again she paused,
and in response to a puzzled glance from General
Gomez, added : " At this moment I think I should
like my name to be—say—Anastasia Edvardova
Karavanskaia, for in that case my orphans would
reap so much the richer harvest."

For already she had determined to send the
money to her Orphan Home in Paris.

It is a curious and occasionally rather disconcerting characteristic of hers that she is satisfied
with four or five hours' sleep during the twenty-
four. It does not matter if she is at rest or at work,
at home or abroad, never under any circumstances
will she consent to go to bed before two or three
o'clock in the morning, and it is not unusual for
her to be out and about by seven. Like all those
whose work depends upon physical fitness, she is
rigorously careful of her diet.

There is no mistaking the sincerity of her love
for England. Certainly she goes each year to Lake
Como for rest and recuperation, but her real home,
and in the very best sense of the word, is the
famous house at Hampstead with which of late
years her name has come to be so closely
associated.

Of all the parties at which I have been present,
the house warming she gave when she first took up
her residence there is by far the most memorable.
Also, I doubt if there have been many occasions
when more people famous in all branches of art,
society, or commerce, have been assembled under
the roof of any one private house. It was then, in

her frank and unassuming pleasure, and in which
was no trace of self-consciousness, that Pavlova
appeared to such great advantage.

Included among her four hundred odd guests
were Princess Bibesco, the Duchess of Rutland, the
Duchess of Marlborough, Lady Crewe, Lady
Katherine and Lady Moyra Cavendish, Mrs. Asquith
(now Lady Oxford), Lady Lytton, Lord Grey, Lady
Maitland, Lady Montgomery, Lady Kimberley,
Lady Isobel Wodehouse, Lady Savile, Lady
Limerick, Lady Muriel Wilson, Lady Violet
Charteris, Lady Howard de Walden, Lord and
Lady Drogheda, Sir William Orpen, Sir Charles
Wyndham, Sir John and Lady Lavery, the Honour-
able Maurice Baring, Sir William and Lady Younger,
Sir Alfred Butt, Lena Ashwell, Mr. and Mrs. Dennis
Eadie, Mr. and Mrs. Robin Legge, Vaughan
Williams, and Netta Syrett.

It was an ideal summer day, and it was after
her temporary absence, during which the guests
assembled on the lawn, that Pavlova sprung
a surprise which must have been as delightful to
her own sense of artistry as unquestionably it
was to the happiness of those in whose honour it
was arranged. For suddenly, without a word of
warning, from every bush which surrounds the
lawn crept dainty gnomes and still daintier nymphs.
And then, at some hidden signal, they danced
about a great tree, and when the dance was at its
height the thick foliage of that tree rustled with
more than the stirring of the summer breeze, and
—Pavlova dropped from the branches into the very

midst of their revels, and danced " The Sylph " as only rarely I had seen her dance it.

At that time there was at Ivy House one of the few authentic ghosts of which I have personal first-hand knowledge. Frequently, when there was any particular press of work, Pavlova would have dressmakers to the house, where it was not unknown for them to work until far into the dawn. Upon several occasions these women reported to her that in the still hours, when they knew that every member of the household was in bed and asleep, they had heard the unmistakable sound of footsteps overhead and the opening and closing of doors.

At first Pavlova dismissed the story as imagination, attributing it to the strain of unduly long working hours. When, however, Clustine, her ballet master, who slept a night in the house, enquired the next morning at breakfast who it was he had heard leave the house in the small hours, and she knew quite well that no one at all had done so, it gave her furiously to think. Entire conviction came when eventually she heard the sounds for herself. Thus it was that the ever-imperturbable M. Dandré was left the only sceptic under her roof. And then, one night, Pavlova and he stayed chatting in the study until much later than usual, and when at last the light was turned off and they were on the point of leaving the room, Pavlova took him by the hand, and with her finger on her lips motioned him to silence.

" Now," she said. " Listen ! "

Sure enough, from the hall, came the tramp, tramp of those ghostly footsteps, until even Dandré was convinced that the house was haunted.

The curious and inexplicable thing about it was that after two years of intermittent manifestation the sounds ceased as abruptly as they had commenced, and from that time to this there have been no signs of their return.

I do not know if prominent artists in other branches of the theatre are subject to the infliction of poetry from their admirers, but with Pavlova it has happened frequently to be the inspiration for this form of self-expression. As might be expected, the very large majority of these efforts are amateur in the extreme, and more often than not purely banal. Indeed, of the many hundred verses which have been written in her honour, I remember only two sets which have succeeded in arousing in her a responsive chord.

The first of these was printed anonymously in the *Calcutta Statesman* during her Indian tour of 1922. It ran as follows :

PAVLOVA

" A gesture, a sweep of the arms, a turn of the head
She dances, and concord arises and discord is dead,
Here is no lyric half-written—no vision half-blurred,
No theme killed and muffled in marble, no music half heard.
Here is a poem incarnate—the flight of a bird.

Colour and line and music and metre and stone
May capture a mood, but she with her body alone

Captures all moods, showing how to the body belong
Colour and line and metre and marble and song.

Work that transfigures the worker shall ever survive ;
Pavlova lives in her dancing—O keep her alive :
Cherish in heart or in hand or in jubilant feet—
In the body's rich fluency cherish, eternal and sweet,
The soul of the body she dances—the poem complete."

But it was a poem which came to her from a
cottage in Aberdeenshire that moved her to a
depth such as I witnessed over no other incident
during the years of our association.

This is how the verses run :

TO PAVLOVA

" Your face I've never seen nor have I held your hand,
　　But oft I hear your name and I beheld a gleam
　　In love's dear eyes that seemed to stray awhile
　　O'er hills afar and like a golden dream
　　Methought I saw a vision of your face,
　　So full of sweetness, purity and grace.

　　This soul of mine doth often wander far,
　　Its deepest thoughts only myself can tell.
　　I often bind the perfume of a flower
　　Into my heart, and let the keen sweet smell
　　Carry me like a barque that drifts upon a stream ;
　　And there alone I find my hope supreme.

　　Dear friend, I frame my thoughts to-day on you,
　　And hope that they will cheer, and may they bring
　　Sweet dreams to you from the veiled skies
　　Where oft I wander, and alone I sing
　　Of royal splendours and of stars sublime
　　As I move slowly o'er the Bridge of Time."

The value of this poem lies much, I think, in the

letter which accompanied it, and which ran as follows :

" DEAR MISS PAVLOVA,

I sincerely hope that you will like this poem which I have dedicated to you, as I have heard so much about you but can never see you because I am blind.

Yours faithfully,

VERNON HORNE."

That tribute finds now a resting place in the little shrine at Ivy House wherein are treasured those things which because they cannot be bought for money are, of all, the most precious in our lives and hearts.

These first chapters, I would explain, are for the purpose that the reader may have some knowledge of the inner life and character of the woman who is their inspiration. In them I have attempted to show that in reality the art of Pavlova is but the medium of expression for a strong and unique personality, and one which has in it just that little leaven of human weakness without which no one of us can be wholly lovable.

Strength ever begets more of respect than of love. In her complexity Pavlova begets both in full measure and brimming over.

Though, sad to say, our professional association is at an end, our friendship yet remains strong and enduring. This applies equally to the calm, imperturbable, and loyal M. Dandré. To Pavlova the art and the inspiration ; to him perhaps the harder part of standing as buffer between her and the constant friction inseparable from incessant travel amid strangers and strange lands. It is M. Dandré who is Chief-of-Staff, who plans the campaigns, decides upon the works to be performed, finds the composers, scene and costume designers, arranges the salaries, conducts the finance. He is the wise father-confessor of the company, the understanding counsellor and friend of every man and girl who through the years has travelled beneath the Pavlova banner.

As I look back I find that by some strange process of the subconscious I never can think of Pavlova but that instantly my thoughts turn to the lilies of the valley with which she loves to surround herself. Odour is memory's greatest stimulant, so that, conversely, the scent of these flowers never reaches me but that some picture of Pavlova in one or other of the many settings in which I have known her arises before the eyes of my mind.

And so it is that now when she comes to London and I set out to greet her, always I carry these flowers in my hand, for I know that with them I shall win the rare smile which only they have power to conjure. Her own house is filled with their fragrance.

And so, I think, are the sacred places of her heart.

CHAPTER IV

MY first impression of America was one of complete bewilderment, though, as nine of my sixteen years with Pavlova were spent there, it was a feeling I had ample opportunity of overcoming. Nor, once I obtained a better understanding of the people and customs, did it take me long to appreciate at its true value the fundamental soundness which is the keynote of this great country.

It cannot be denied, however, that to the stranger America presents the most amazing contrasts. How, indeed, could it be otherwise, in a country where in at least one State it is illegal to smoke a cigarette in the street, and where in other parts there is so much licence ? Even since the Volstead Act I have witnessed more drunkenness in Broadway on one Saturday night than can be seen in other great capitals in a month.

Though more of outward seeming than actuality, America conveys the impression, to a stranger, of having one law for the rich and another for the poor, and that the power of money is something very nearly approaching an absolute monarchy. An instance of this occurred during my very first week in New York, and transpired, of all good times and places, during a dress rehearsal

AN INTIMATE REHEARSAL. (METROPOLITAN OPERA HOUSE)

Names from left to right :—Myself, Pianist, Ivan Clustine, Anna Pavlova, Alexander Volinine.

I was conducting at the Metropolitan Opera
House.

While we were engaged with the most important
scene in the ballet the manager's secretary tapped
me on the shoulder.

" Sorry, Maestro, but I'm afraid you'll have to
stop the rehearsal," he announced apologetically.

" Stop ? " I repeated blankly. " Why ? "

" We need the stage for Mr. Otto Kahn to hold
an audition for two or three vocalists," he said.

" Who is Mr. Otto Kahn," I demanded,
" that he should interfere in the middle of a dress
rehearsal ? "

I was young at the time, and knew not what
blasphemy I spoke.

With later knowledge I wonder that I was not
lynched forthwith. My question was equivalent,
in pre-war days, to a German recruit enquiring
who was the Kaiser Wilhelm.

" Young man," the secretary said impressively,
" let me tell you that without Mr. Otto Kahn
there would be no Metropolitan Opera House ;
Madame Pavlova would not be here, and *you*
would not be here. If it comes to a showdown,
Mr. Otto Kahn *is* the Metropolitan Opera House."

And though at the time the situation struck
me as an amazing one, I was later to discover
what a substantial groundwork of fact the claim
was based upon.

So far as the Metropolitan Opera House was
concerned, the great financier exercised a benevolent autocracy that was one of the greatest assets

E

in American art. Nor was this influence confined
to music, though it was to that House, and at his
own expense, that he brought the wonderful
Sistine Choir from Rome for a series of concerts ;
as, also, he was the medium for the presentation
to New York audiences of the company from the
Moscow Art Theatre. In addition, and perhaps
of more importance still, it was through him that
the Metropolitan Museum of Art was founded in
New York—than which there could be no greater
monument to the patriotism and love of the
beautiful of Mr. Otto Kahn.

Though perhaps not so evident on the surface,
the line of demarcation between the classes is far
more broad in America than is the case in any
European country. But whereas in many of the
latter the gift of high birth may still be contributory
to social eminence, in the United States it is wealth
that counts as the great standard of success.

With the gospel of the democratic ideal as the
keystone of national education, reaction against
the newer doctrine is natural and inevitable.
Speaking generally, this is displayed by an insistence
upon social equality which not always is distinguished by reciprocal understanding on the part
of the protagonist concerned.

Already I have referred to my experience with
the Musicians' Union, which is both typical of
what I mean and of the autocrats of a similar
type with which the stranger is everywhere confronted.

While anxious always to conform to the customs

of any country in which I may find myself, even to
the extent of addressing my waiter as " MISTER,"
I do at least expect a similar courtesy in return.
In one particular case, however, which occurred
at the best hotel in a city which shall be nameless,
we were inflicted with a waiter who, upon taking
the orders, and referring to Pavlova, enquired
ingenuously what " that woman " would eat.
Individual male members of our party he spoke of
as " that man."

It was not, however, until he left to fulfil the
orders that the true humour of the situation was
brought home to us, for stuck in a silver frame in
the centre of the table was a card of which the
following is an exact reproduction :

YOUR WAITER IS
MR. DAVE JULIAN
NO. 13.

During the whole of our tours, both in the
United States and Mexico, the Musicians' Union
were a continual thorn in our sides. Their power
was absolute, and they used it unsparingly, oblivious
of our interests, convenience, or even of the elementary principles of everyday courtesy.

Illustrative of this was an incident which occurred
at Acron, Ohio.

Speaking generally our organisation was perfect,
as, indeed, considering the conditions under which
we travelled, it was absolutely essential that it
should be. It is in this respect that I should
like to pay tribute to the efficiency with which,

apart from one or two exceptional and untoward circumstances that could not possibly be foreseen, our not inconsiderable transport was worked. There was a smoothness and rapidity of service in America that was unexcelled by any other country through which we travelled.

All told our company consisted of no less than eighty people, besides which we carried scenery for thirty productions, and travelled two hundred and eighty trunks of costumes. For the accommodation of so many people, and so vast an amount of material, our train consisted of eight coaches—five day coaches and three Pullman sleepers. Of these latter Pavlova and the principals occupied one, the members of the ballet the second, and the orchestra the third.

On this particular occasion then, when, after a particularly strenuous performance at the local theatre, we arrived on the railway platform in the small hours of the morning, it was to be greeted by a polite and apologetic stationmaster with the information that one of the Pullmans had broken down, and though every effort had been used it had been found impossible to replace it.

Under the circumstances Pavlova took it for granted that the musicians would put up no very stenuous objection to occupying one of the day coaches, particularly as there were no ladies travelling in their car; in any case it was their custom to sit up playing poker until five or six o'clock each morning.

But to employ their own metaphor there was

"nothing doing." Their contract called for a
Pullman coach for each night of the tour, and they
gave us very definitely to understand that at whatever cost to anyone else they intended that it
should be adhered to, and until it was provided
they refused point-blank to leave the platform.
Eventually, stung to desperation, the Manager
approached Pavlova, who already was comfortably
installed in her drawing-room, and informed her of
the situation.

Pavlova said characteristically : " I refuse to
allow the girls to spend the night in the day coach.
As the position seems unbridgeable, the only thing
to be done is for myself and the principals to suffer
the inconvenience."

Thereupon we loaded ourselves with the night
attire that already was placed in our sleeper, and,
headed by Madame Pavlova herself, filed out of
the Pullman to make room for the orchestra, who
were lined up outside the door, apparently unmoved by the procedure. However, I shall not
readily forget Pavlova's face as she watched the
orchestra climbing into her own private coach,
where they sat up smoking and playing cards until
close upon breakfast-time.

A further example illustrative both of the extreme Puritanism of a certain section of American
society, and of the autocracy we found so disconcerting, occurred in Springfield, Illinois.

Pavlova received word that one of the men of
the company had been taken suddenly ill in his
hotel. Of course she collected me, and we hurried

round at once—nothing could have kept her away.
Arrived at the hotel she enquired the number of
his room, and having ascertained it, took the
elevator straight up. Outside the door, however,
she paused, turning to me : " Maestro, do you mind
slipping down to the flower stand in the lobby and
buying some roses," she said, and passed inside
the room.

She had not been chatting three minutes with
the patient, however, before without leave or
ceremony the door was burst open, and in dashed
the hotel detective.

" You've gotta go," he said. " Right now."

Pavlova looked at him in the utmost amazement.

" Go ? " she repeated dazedly " Go where ? "

" Anywhere out of this room," he replied sternly.
" If your friend wants to entertain women in his
bedroom, he'd better beat it out of this ho-tel.
We don't stand for that sort of thing here ! "

And, too dazed even for protest, Pavlova left.

No one who travels constantly about the world
but can fail to be struck by the varying methods of
the Customs authorities in the different countries.
In America, particularly, they are a very uncertain
quantity indeed. One's reception, of course, varies
with the type of official who takes one in hand.
Once assured of your good faith, some of them are
pleasant and easy-going ; others appear to take
a delight in turning all your most cherished possessions out of carefully packed trunks and bags,
and leaving them distributed about the floor of
the shed—a pleasing custom occasionally em-

barrassing to ladies! One man I got hold of on my first visit was of average good humour, but suffered with an apparently ingrained mistrust of human nature.

One fact of which I was unaware is that there is a heavy duty on old and valuable violins. Included in my kit was an instrument which, however venerable in appearance, was of recent make and quite inexpensive, and to which my Customs man pointed a menacing finger.

"How much did that stand you for?" he demanded.

"Three pounds," I replied, which surprisingly enough happened to be the literal truth.

His expression registered incredulity, and the conviction that I was trying to "put one over" him.

"Fifteen dollars!" he exclaimed. "I guess you can't get away with a tale like that." He picked up and carefully scrutinised the instrument, which I could see instinctively he knew nothing whatever about. "This is a valooable fiddle," he pronounced. "I guess you've got another think coming about how much they stung you for it."

"That fiddle," I repeated gently, "cost me just under fifteen dollars in your money. Three pounds, to be accurate."

Not too gently the man replaced the instrument in its case.

"You've gotta *show* me," he said derisively. "I'm from Missouri."

I am not easily annoyed, but on this occasion
I thought it up to me to call his bluff.

"All right," I said. "You say that it's worth
far more than fifteen dollars, so that if you pay
that for it you've got a bargain. Give me the
money and the fiddle's yours."

He looked hard at me for a moment, saw that I
meant exactly what I said, and then handed me
the violin case.

"Nothin' doin'!" he said.

I'm sorry to say that violin is still in my possession.

Writing of losing my temper, one of the few
occasions in my life when I really did so, was in
Los Angeles. Usually I find it much more difficult
to give way to temper than to retain it. But this
particular occasion is one of the few when actually
I saw red.

The beginning of the affair happened in San
Francisco. On our opening night I noticed in the
stalls, close behind me, a man who appeared to be
even more enthusiastic about the performance
than were the rest of the audience; as a matter
of fact he was a little too demonstrative.

The following night there he was again in the
same seat, and the next night and the next, and
the more often he saw the performance the greater
appeared his appreciation. Then he began sending
cigars for the men of the company, and flowers
and chocolates for the girls. Finally he struck up
an acquaintance with myself.

He was a most charming and delightful fellow,

named Robert Martin, and hailed from El Paso ; cheery, warm-hearted, and generous to a degree. It was not long before he became *persona grata* with everyone in the company. He occupied the same seat in the stalls every single night during our stay in San Francisco.

When we left for Los Angeles and he came to see us off from the station, he seemed terribly distressed to think that this was our good-bye.

Finally, however, he brightened.

" Say," he said, " it's only three hundred miles to Los Angeles. What's to stop me coming down and looking you up there ? "

This is what so many people feel it incumbent to say in bidding a theatrical company farewell, that I did not regard the suggestion very seriously.

" Glad to see you," I said warmly. " Drop in any old time, and there'll always be a welcome for you."

" You bet your life I will," he said.

Nevertheless, when we had been playing in Los Angeles for a week, with no signs of our El Paso friend, I was more regretful than surprised ; I had not thought for a moment that he would feel it necessary to keep his tentative engagement. Then one night I was told that there was a gentleman waiting in my dressing-room, and going there during the first interval I was delighted to find Bob Martin awaiting me.

We had been chatting for perhaps five minutes, when something occurred that was so utterly incredible and bizarre that for a moment it left

me without power of thought or speech. For the
door burst open, and without a word of explanation,
in marched the stage doorkeeper—who was one
of the largest and strongest men I ever saw—
seized Bob Martin by the collar and the slack of
the trousers, and ran him out of the room and
down the corridor which led to the street exit.

When I had recovered from my amazement
sufficiently to move, I rushed after the pair, and
not without difficulty succeeded in rescuing my
friend.

At that moment I was more angry than ever I
have been before or since. In no measured terms
I demanded an explanation.

The doorkeeper said, merely, that he had been
acting only upon instructions. When I asked
him upon whose, he replied, " The manager's."
I was unable, however, to elicit from him which of
the three managers it was ; the business manager,
the stage manager, or the publicity manager, the
last named of whom, owing to travelling ahead of
the company, had few personal relations with
individual members or their friends.

I learnt afterwards that the theatre officials
had been pestered very much with strangers at
the back of the stage, and that a ukase had gone
forth that under no circumstances were any more
to be admitted, and that if by chance any should
gain entrance they were immediately to be ejected.
Bob Martin, as had been his custom in San Francisco, had marched past the stage doorkeeper
without a word, stood for a moment in the wings,

and because the interval was approaching, had
gone down to wait for me in my dressing-room.

While he had been standing in the wings,
however, he had been noticed, as I discovered
afterwards, by the publicity manager, and as
all the company with whom my friend was
acquainted happened at the moment to be on the
stage, there was no one to give any satisfactory
reply as to who this stranger was. Hence, without
troubling himself further, the publicity manager
had instructed the stage doorkeeper to " put that
guy outside."

When, however, the official realised that in this
particular case he had bitten off rather more than
he could chew he, in co-operation with his two
colleagues, proceeded to engineer a conspiracy of
silence as to with whom lay responsibility for the
order of ejectment—a policy they considered as
effective counteraction against my absolute refusal
to conduct the orchestra until the guilty party had
made adequate apology to my friend.

But to use their own metaphor the scheme cut
no ice with me. It was certain that one of those
three officials was responsible, and I had no hesitation in delivering an ultimatum to the effect that
as apparently the one who had given the order
was not in possession of the common decency to
own up, then the performance would not continue
until Robert Martin was apologised to, and in
terms which I myself would dictate, by each one
of the three managers concerned.

As already the moment had passed when the

curtain should have gone up there were, of course, the most frenzied protests. But at that moment it was not protests I was interested in. What I wanted, and what I was determined to have before I took my seat in the orchestra, was a joint apology to Robert Martin.

Then they said that they would report the matter to Pavlova, though had they known her a little longer they might well have hesitated in carrying out their threat. Actually, however, by this time the unduly prolonged interval, and certain indications of unrest which quite clearly penetrated to the back of the stage from the audience, had made her aware that something was wrong, and she sent from her dressing-room to enquire what it was.

She was at her iciest as she listened to the explanation of the three managers. When it came to her turn to speak she told them very definitely that she associated herself in every way with the stand I had taken; that Robert Martin was a friend of hers, and that even if this had not been the case an insult to a friend of her musical director's was an insult to herself; that in my place she would have taken exactly the same course as I had done. The performance would not recommence until the joint apology was forthcoming.

There, then, was the *impasse*. It was now well over half an hour past the time when normally the curtain should have reascended, and there was not even the usual soporific of the orchestra to help keep the audience in hand. And a Los Angeles audience with a grievance is not an easy crowd to

handle. Even then the shoutings and stampings
showed that it would not be many more moments
before there was something doing.

They had to climb down ; there was nothing else
for it. Jointly and severally those three managers
delivered a humble and abject oration of apology,
at my dictation, to the by now highly embarrassed
Robert Martin. The moment the last syllable
had left their lips, I hurried into the orchestra to
join my intrigued musicians—after an interval of
thirty-five minutes instead of ten.

The sequel was not unamusing. It was our last
performance in Los Angeles, and immediately after
the curtain fell we had to pack and hurry down
to the station.

To my surprise there was no sign of Bob Martin;
nor, for that matter, was there any sign of the
three managers.

Pavlova was equally mystified. Never before
had Bob Martin lost an opportunity of exchanging
even a few words with her ; it was inconceivable
that he should fail her at this last minute.

And then, just as we were on the point of boarding
the train, through the murk of the far end of the
platform we perceived the silhouettes of four male
figures advancing towards us in attitudes of closest
kinship. At one moment their arms would be
interlocked, at the next one figure would detach
himself from the group to execute a few steps of
some quaint old-world dance. As the quartette
approached us it was in a combined effort to
reproduce Pavlova's own " Bacchanal."

It was Martin and the three managers—the first-named no longer " Robert " but " Bob," as to him the others were Charley and Bill and Harry.

Wine may be a mocker, but it certainly does bring people together !

CHAPTER V

ANOTHER intensely interesting and fascinating personality we met in San Francisco was Charley Young, the son of a wealthy newspaper proprietor. In the whole of the sixteen years I was with the company, indeed, he was the most universally popular of all the friends we made.

He was a most enthusiastic and devoted protagonist of the ballet, coming to the theatre practically every night of our stay, and as he had plenty of spare time on his hands it was his delight to show San Francisco to any of the company who liked to share his leisure. He was, too, like so very many of his countrymen, particularly generous and hospitable, and the presents he showered on us all must have cost him a considerable amount of money.

But it was not the material benefits reaped from knowing him which mattered, it was the real charm of his society and the cheery wit and good humour with which he was blessed that counted so much with us all. Actually he made such a big impression that after we left the city it was no uncommon thing to hear the girls counting off the days to their return, " and then we shall see Charley again."

Alas! that reunion was destined never to

materialise. Adventurous as he was cheerful, Charley went into thedesert hunting big game, an expedition which proved disastrous. Tracking some animal or other he lost his way; his water gave out so that he was obliged to drink the unclean water of a desert pool. Typhoid ensued, from which he did not recover.

And then there was the late Victor Herbert, the Irish-American composer, whose operas were, and are, a household word throughout the whole of the United States, and whom I met first in New York, and whose work I was more than once privileged to conduct.

I rarely knew a man whose joy in living was so vivid, nor one so universally beloved of his fellows. One of the most striking sides of his character was a generosity which rendered it almost a personal affront for anyone who happened to be in his company to offer to pay for anything at all. Neither the number present, nor how often or recently any of them had enjoyed his society, made any difference whatever; his insistence upon the *rôle* of paymaster-general never flagged under any circumstances.

It was the same with the largesse it was his habit to distribute promiscuously to any private or public servant who happened to have performed the smallest service for him.

It was his habit to carry a roll of bills " thick enough to choke a mule," and none of a lesser denomination than five dollars, and for which he refused resolutely to accept change. Thus it was with one of these that he would pay a twenty-five cent taxi fare; it was the same for a glass of ice-water or a shoe-shine in his hotel.

With other and lesser men this system of whole-sale distribution might have smacked of ostentation; Victor Herbert did not know the meaning of the word. He gave, not to attract attention, but because it was his greatest pleasure in life to bring happiness to others. He made an enormous amount of money, and, with him, money was meant only to be spent or given away—the latter for preference.

For a little time I was his musical director, and so was brought into close personal touch with him. Thus I am able to write from personal experience that his generosity and charm were not confined to his social life; he was exactly the same in his business relationships.

I remember upon one occasion being dissatisfied with the trumpeter of the orchestra, and suggesting to Herbert that we made a change, to which he agreed without hesitation. A day or two later he rang me up on the telephone.

" Don't bother about looking for another trumpeter," he said. " I've found one, and I want you to come around to my apartment straight away to see him."

" There's no occasion to take up your time," I protested. " Just send him round to me."

But this Victor Herbert would not consent to. For a reason he refused resolutely to elucidate he was insistent the interview should take place at his own apartment. Knowing him as I did,

F

moreover, I was able to realise that he had some good motive for this somewhat unusual procedure. So I hurried round to keep the appointment. And there, besides Victor Herbert, I discovered the applicant for the vacant orchestral position, awaiting me.

Although in his professional capacity he seemed eminently qualified for the post, there yet was nothing about this latter which struck me either as unusual or remarkable, so that I was more at a loss than ever to discover Victor Herbert's purpose in putting himself to such trouble. Presently, however, he turned to me, hardly suppressed delight in his eyes.

" I'll bet you ten dollars you can't guess what this gentleman's name is," he said.

I thought of all the unlikely surnames that, on the spur of the moment, I could summon to my mind. All were hopelessly wide of the mark. Finally he waved his hand towards the grinning trumpeter.

" Allow me to present you," he said importantly, " to—*Beethoven !* "

And actually that was the musician's name; so far as he could discover, moreover, the remote but sole descendant of the original and illustrious bearer of it. And ever after it was delightful, when anything transpired on the stage which offended Victor Herbert's critical musical ear, to hear him say gravely to the offender :

" My dear sir (or madame, as the case may have been), if you knew whom you had listening to you, I feel sure you would do so much better.''

Naturally the artist would require to know who this illustrious individual was. Then would Victor Herbert demand that the trumpeter should stand upright in his place.

'' Beethoven ! '' he would announce, with a grandiloquent wave of his hand.

Small wonder that Victor Herbert was so universally beloved. May the soil rest lightly upon this gallant and fascinating artist and Irishman.

When an artist of any importance visits Los Angeles there is no difficulty in becoming acquainted with the stars of Hollywood; for they make a point of visiting the performance, and sending their cards to the dressing-room at its close, a custom which not only dispenses with formality but opens wide the door of hospitality to the visitor.

It was in this way that we met Douglas Fairbanks and the delightful Mary Pickford, who invited us up to tea on the following Sunday afternoon.

As our car drove up to the door of their very beautiful house, where both were on the steps awaiting us, it was not difficult to discern that for once our host was not entirely at his ease. For the usually immaculate Douglas was suffering from a three days' growth of beard. It appeared that three or four days previously in one of those athletic performances for which his pictures are renowned, he had hurt his hand so badly as to be unable to use a razor, a condition which resulted in a very obvious self-consciousness, for if during that afternoon he apologised for his facial disorder once he must have done so half a dozen times. It seemed literally to be preying on his mind.

Nevertheless we had a most delightful time, one that was rendered all the more pleasant by the manifest happiness of our hosts. Whatever may be the married relations of other Hollywood stars, there is no doubt whatever as to the complete and utter harmony in the lives of Douglas Fairbanks and the World's Sweetheart, the latter as charming and dainty in her own home as so many millions throughout the world have come to know her on the " silver screen."

It was in Los Angeles, too, that I met and became friends with Charlie Chaplin, a friendship which remains unbroken to the time of writing.

A mystic, fascinating, and illusive personality ! Cultured, dreamy ; musician and actor ; he represents the artistic temperament to a greater degree than anyone I know, and like all great artists his moods alternate strangely between fair weather and gloom. At one time he is on the heights, freakish and the comedian born, at others sunk to a depression from which only the natural reactions of his own temperament are able to arouse him.

And the versatility of the man is simply amazing. He is most deeply read, and possesses a knowledge of philosophy which would assure respect for his opinions in any literary circle in the world. Less generally known, I think, is his talent as a musician ; he plays the violin quite exceptionally well, and, more extraordinary still, plays it left-handed. His knowledge of opera and symphony is equally surprising ; there is hardly one of any moment from which he cannot whistle excerpts.

It was inevitable that while we were in Los Angeles he and Pavlova should meet.

After they had been brought together several times Pavlova hired a small Italian restaurant, from which, for the time being, the public was excluded, with Chaplin as guest of the evening. But it was he who provided the entertainment.

He was in the most amazing good spirits that night. As there were no facilities for Pavlova to dance, he announced with perfect gravity his intention that the guests should not go home without receiving an entirely authentic impression of her art and methods, as interpreted by himself.

And in a space provided by the expedient of clearing the tables from the centre of the room, he gave his conception of how Pavlova would dance the " Swan " and " Salome " dances.

The latter, in particular, was one of the funniest things I have seen, and incidentally the most amazingly clever ; burlesque carried to a perfection which sublimated its extravagance to the point of genius.

When with his advent the silent drama gained this outstanding comedian, the vaudeville stage was denuded of its greatest potential humorist.

Another occasion when he shone was when he drove twenty-five of our girls into the country, and, as the only man present, devoted himself during the picnic which came at the end of the journey to a series of antics which kept them in a state of helpless laughter until it was time to go home.

Some of my most pleasant recollections are of the Athletic Club at Los Angeles—that wonderful institution, with its palatial swimming pool, library, Turkish and eucalyptus baths, and its splendid hospitality to any stranger of moment who happens temporarily to be in the city, and where each evening it was my habit to foregather with Chaplin and Sir Herbert Tree when that great actor was playing for D. W. Griffiths.

It was curious how I came to meet Tree. It was during the War—in the summer of 1916 to be exact, and the Pavlova Company was temporarily disbanded. Some of the girls Pavlova obtained engagements for elsewhere, to others she paid a retaining fee until such time as the company was reassembled; had there been one of them who she was not assured was free from financial embarrassment she would not have had a happy moment.

In the meanwhile Pavlova herself, M. Dandré, and one or two of the principals had gone to Los Angeles for a holiday. I myself was at something of a loose end in New York.

And then one day I received a cable from Dandré which must have cost him a small fortune. In it he explained that Mr. Behymer—the greatest impresario west of Chicago, and who, incidentally, commenced his career as a street-car conductor—had pointed out to Pavlova what extremely bad business it was to burden herself with the cost of a

long holiday in an expensive city like Los Angeles
when, by giving only one performance a week
the whole vacation might be enjoyed free of
cost.

Having with her at least the nucleus of a company the idea appealed to Pavlova as sound, and
my cable of recall was the result.

M. Dandré met me at the station and drove me
to the Hollywood Hotel. Walking across the
vestibule I could see Pavlova and her party in the
dining-room, and was able to distinguish every
figure but one, the latter a broad-shouldered man
seated next to Pavlova, and with his back to me.
Curiously, that back was strongly reminiscent of
M. Dandré himself.

" It can't be you," I said to him as he turned
from the desk where he had been arranging for
my room, " because you're here with me. Who
then, is it ? "

" Ah ! " said M. Dandré, " that is a little surprise in store for you," and taking me directly into
the dining-room presented me to Sir Herbert
Beerbohm Tree.

We sat next to each other at dinner, and seemed
to hit it off from the first. In the course of conversation he explained that he was under contract
for—I believe—seven thousand dollars a week, to
play for D. W. Griffiths, in fulfilment of which
arrangement he had come over with his daughter
Iris, and had taken a furnished bungalow a little
down the road from the hotel. She, however, had
gone on a short visit to the Bahamas, and Sir

Herbert was chafing pretty badly under the separation, for above all things he hated being alone.

When, then, it came to his knowledge that Pavlova was so near to him, he made a point of introducing himself to her, and asked that she would relieve the tedium by allowing him to dine at her table each evening, to which, of course, she had gladly assented.

Just at this time, he explained, he was rather perturbed in his mind. The day after his arrival he had called upon D. W. Griffiths. For some considerable time they discussed everything but the business in hand.

Eventually Tree asked what it was that Griffiths wanted him to play.

To his amazement Griffiths's reply was :

" I don't know, Sir Herbert. Have you thought of anything ? "

It was a long while before the great English actor could be brought to realise that actually he had been engaged at something like two hundred pounds a day to appear in a film of which even the subject had not yet been arranged.

" Of course I'm under contract," Tree said to me that night, " but it seems an amazing thing, and I'm rather more than interested to discover what Griffiths's idea is when the contract commences."

Had he known D. W. Griffiths as well as later both he and myself came to know and understand his methods, he would not have given the matter a second thought But surely enough on the Saturday morning a cheque arrived for the first week's salary, and the week following, with still nothing done, a further cheque for a similar amount. I think Tree was the most puzzled man in the whole of the North American Continent.

That was only typical of Griffiths, to whom the cost of anything he really wanted was the very last consideration to count.

An instance of this lavishness was when he wished to use forty-eight bars of Strauss's symphonic poem, "A Hero's Life," for "Intolerance," a performance which at a liberal estimate would have lasted about a minute and a half. As the time was in the middle of the War and Strauss himself in Munich, it was necessary to cable to him via Holland to enquire for terms, a matter in itself of not inconsiderable expense.

The reply, when eventually it came, was a demand for one hundred dollars per performance— and it must be remembered that when the film was released the probability was that it would be shown pretty well throughout the whole habitable globe.

To this Griffiths actually consented. Before, however, the matter was definitely arranged he happened to mention it to me, and it was only after considerable discussion that I persuaded him not to sign the contract. Eventually Liszt's " The Huns' Battle " was substituted, upon which there was no royalty payable.

While Griffiths was engaged in filming this same " Intolerance " he was anxious to obtain some

real Persian folk songs. After scouring the whole
of Los Angeles a *pukka* Persian woman was discovered who, for a consideration, consented to
whistle a round dozen peasant songs of her native
country, but as Griffiths did not like any one
of them he commissioned me to find him
another twelve, which eventually I succeeded in
doing.

Some months later when I was in New York and
happening to be glancing through Schirmer's music
store at the corner of Fifth Avenue and Twenty-
third Street, I discovered, included in a book selling
at seventy-five cents, all the songs for which
Griffiths had paid the Persian woman three hundred
dollars each time she whistled !

Writing of film stars reminds me of one of the
few occasions when I have seen Pavlova really
disconcerted.

When she was in London she and I visited a
theatre where Charles Bryant was playing in " Bella
Donna," and she was so impressed with his performance that at intervals over the next few months
she referred to him so continually that at last I
began to chaff her unmercifully. Eventually it
became one of those friendly jokes we so often
enjoyed together.

It was while we were playing at the Century
Opera House in New York nearly a year later
that Nazimova's card was sent up to Pavlova's
dressing-room, and as the two were old acquaintances in Russia, naturally the reunion was a
delightful one.

After chatting for some little time, however, Nazimova got up out of her chair.

" Don't go, please ! " Pavlova pleaded, reluctant so soon to part from a friend with whom she had so much in common.

" As a matter of fact," Nazimova explained, " I've stayed too long already. You see, my husband is waiting for me at the stage door."

" *Why* didn't you say so before," Pavlova exclaimed, and turned to me. " Maestro, please go down and ask him to come up at once."

" But how shall I know which is he ? " I enquired of the great screen actress.

" I don't think you'll have any difficulty," Nazimova said, " because I expect he'll be the only man who's in evening dress."

Accordingly I hurried down, experienced but small difficulty in collecting my man, and brought him up to the dressing-room.

" Allow me," Nazimova said to Pavlova, " to present my husband."

Pavlova's face as she turned to greet her guest was a study. Then, with a quick glance at me we both broke into peals of laughter—for Nazimova's husband was Charles Bryant.

It must be added that when the reason of our laughter was explained to the mystified couple they seemed to enter into the joke with an enjoyment at least as keen as our own.

But to come back to Tree. With one performance a week, and that a matinée, my work was a sinecure, so that each evening I was free to enjoy his company. After dinner it was our habit to drive to the Athletic Club, and we used not to be there very long before Chaplin joined us. And there we would sit until two or three o'clock in the morning, for apart from Pavlova herself I do not remember anyone so entirely reluctant to go to bed as Tree. Nevertheless they were most memorable nights, with Tree discussing in that deep resonant voice of his any and every subject which happened to flit through his versatile and assimilative brain, and from angles which would have occurred to no one but himself; Chaplin meanwhile humming or whistling tunes of Schumann, Elgar, or Brahms. Tree and he grew to be close friends, and it used to delight me to watch them marching down the street arm in arm together, they were so beautifully reminiscent of Don Quixote and Sancho Panza in real life.

On those evenings, even when Charlie left us, Tree would never consent to go to bed without a further sitting in his own bungalow. To fill in the leisure which was so irksome to him, he was writing a book, extracts from which he loved to read aloud to me until the sun shone clear above the heavens. The novel was entitled *Nothing Matters*. I do not know if it ever saw the light, but it was amazingly clever and entertaining.

But kind and hospitable as was everybody in Los Angeles, I never was quite able to reconcile myself to the social atmosphere of Hollywood—a place where it is said that the only permanent job is that of bridesmaid to a film star. Certainly, so

far as I could gather, the marital relations of many
of those most prominent in the world of the screen
are like Sam Weller's knowledge of London—
extensive and peculiar. Illustrative of this I
remember one perfectly ludicrous incident of which
Charlie, Tree, and myself were intrigued spectators.

There was at that time two film performers
whose married life, so far as I was able to gather,
had been one long drawn-out battle, and who in
spite of the good offices of various friends had not
quite succeeded in sinking their differences. So
with their consent, and in order to clinch what
appeared to be a conciliatory mood on the part of
both, Charlie Chaplin arranged what was intended as a " Reunion Party " in honour of the
couple.

At first everything went merrily as the proverbial
marriage bell. There was an elaborate supper at
which the healths of the couple were drunk with
musical honours, and to the accompaniment of
loud and enthusiastic cheering. And after the
supper Charlie Chaplin set himself to entertain his
guests.

He was in the highest spirits at the success of
his party, and that night he excelled himself. He
danced as only he can dance ; he fooled as only he
can fool ; and played the fiddle as merrily. Suddenly
I noticed a look of rather anxious enquiry pass
across his singularly expressive face, and watched
him as his glance travelled from one to the other
of his guests. Then, rather hurriedly, he stepped
out from a corner table where he had been chatting.

" Where is So-and-so," he demanded, mentioning the name of the husband.

To the end of my life I shall never forget his face when he was told that, following a passionate renewal of hostilities with his wife, his chief gentleman guest had tempestuously left ! This was the only time I ever saw Chaplin disgruntled ; not so much at the expense he had been put to, though this was considerable, as at the absurd anti-climax.

It was later, in Pittsburg, where both were appearing, that I had the pleasure of effecting an introduction between Pavlova and Sybil Thorndike.

My old friend, Lewis Casson, was playing in the same Frohman Company as his wife, and the meeting was arranged between our two selves. The difficulty was as to the *venue*. In Pittsburg the hotel dining-rooms, wherein a certain measure of quiet conversation is assured, are closed inexorably as bankers' safes after a certain hour, a custom which entirely ruled out our all having supper together under the usual after-the-show custom. The restaurants, with their blaring jazz bands and enthusiastic dancers, are death and mutilation to any chance of a quiet talk, and the cabarets more so. Eventually it was decided that the only thing for it was to meet at one of the Childs restaurants, where at least a measure of tranquillity would be assured. To the uninitiated I would explain that " Childs " are the " Lyons " of America.

The meeting duly took place after the performance, as arranged, and without waste of time we drove directly to the particular branch of Childs we had picked out as most suitable for our purpose.

There, over supper, it was easy to see that the two great artists had succeeded at once in establishing common ground of interest; they hit it off famously. Reminiscences, views, anecdotes were exchanged; mutual friends and their activities discussed; all sense of time forgotten.

When, after two hours, we called for the bill, it was to discover the total for the four of us was exactly a dollar and a quarter—about 5s. 8d. in English money.

It was outside the restaurant, and while engaged in mutual congratulations on an almost ludicrously inexpensive evening, that I discovered Lewis Casson and myself had each left it to the other to dismiss the taxi that had brought us, and that, neither having done so, the driver had waited. At the time the latter drew our attention to his presence the amount registered on the clock was fifteen dollars!

It was near Los Angeles that we encountered one of the few really dangerous experiences of all our World tours, though twice we were fortunate in missing earthquakes, once in Japan, by exactly one year to the day and where the Imperial Theatre at which we played was turned into a heap of ruins, and again in Santa Barbara, where our hotel in which we had stayed was reduced to ashes only four weeks after our departure.

Our Californian adventure, on the other hand, had to do with floods. It was when we travelled

from San Francisco to Los Angeles. We were
warned before leaving the former place that floods
might render the journey impracticable, but decided
to risk it. We found, however, that the warning
had not been exaggerated.

It was one of the darkest nights within my
recollection, and when, with the water up to the
windows of the coaches, we drew slowly to a halt,
the already overstrained nerves of the temperamental Russian members of the company began
to give out. Nor did the fact that our stoppage
was caused by a bridge having been swept away,
and which even then was being patched up to
enable us to pass, tend to reassurance. As the
time approached for us to move, those of the ballet
who were not fervidly muttering prayers were
crossing themselves, and I think only Pavlova's
own coolness saved the situation from developing
into panic.

As it happened, we crossed without mishap, but
that there were very real grounds for alarm was
proved when a little later we learned that the
bridge actually collapsed within a few moments of
the last of our coaches crossing over.

At the Odeon Theatre, St. Louis, on that same
tour, Pavlova had an accident which might have
proved very much more serious than actually it
was.

Speaking generally, she is always practising,
holding that it is the most important principle
upon which perfection is founded, and the only
certain safeguard against accidents. And when I

speak of practising, I do not refer so much to practising on the stage, but to the constant and calculated employment of the necessary muscles in the ordinary course of her daily life—even when walking or talking. She has said many times that she regards this as exercise important equally as her actual stage work.

On this particular occasion, however, something occurred to interfere with her usual routine, so that when she went on to the stage at night she was not able to assume her usual exact muscular control. The result was that during Rubenstein's " Valse Caprice " she slipped a ligament of her leg and went off into a dead faint, hence there was no work for three weeks, and the consequent cancellation of our engagements during that period.

In the whole of the sixteen years of our association that was the only time within my recollection that she went on to the stage not wholly keyed up for her performance, and it was a lesson which she never afterwards permitted herself to forget.

G

CHAPTER VI

IT was in America, at Toledo, Ohio, that for the first and only time in my life I was the victim of a deliberate swindle.

We arrived in the city in the middle of a crime wave which seemed to have gripped the country. In Toledo, for instance, hold-ups at night were as frequent as motor casualties, and we were warned against all kinds of major or minor crimes which might be attempted against us. Hence there is room for wonder at my own victimization.

I remember that I was behind the stage at the time—to be frank I was packing my laundry, and, incidentally, thoroughly immersed in my job. A hatless man with a pen behind his ear and waving some papers in his hand dashed up.

" Say, Mr. Stier," he said, " I've been looking for Mr. Hirsh every place about this durned theatre. Can you give me any line where I can get hold of him ? " Mr. Hirsh being our manager, and the man addressing me by name, lulled any suspicions which otherwise I might have entertained. Actually I took him to be one of the box-office staff.

" What is it you want him for ? " I said.

" It's this way," he said. " The printers have brought to-night's programme and the bill."

That being none of my business, I told him I

98

had no idea where the manager was. The man wandered off and I got on with my job.

Five minutes later he was back, and this time he looked pretty worried.

" Say, Mr. Stier," he said seriously, " I can't find Mr. Hirsh any place, and the guy who brought those programmes says he won't leave 'em unless he gets the money. I'd pay him myself, but I've only got twenty dollars in my roll, and I've given him that, but he's waiting for another twenty."

I should have known better ; printers do not dun the principal theatre in a city as large as Toledo for twenty dollars. However, the amount was trivial, and for all I knew the firm who supplied the programmes made it their policy to cut their prices by insisting upon cash on delivery. To make a long story short I gave them an all the money I happened to have with me, which was eighteen dollars, and went back to my laundry basket, forgetting the incident until it was time to go home. Then, on my way to the exit, I looked in at Hirsh's office to reclaim my money.

To my astonishment he met my demand with a look of blank dismay.

" But, Maestro," he objected, " we never ordered any programmes. All our printing is done in New York."

There were several people in the office, all, of course, hugely delighted at the trick that had been played on me. In the middle of the laughter in came Dandré.

" Oh, by the way, Mr. Hirsh," he remarked

casually, " while I'm here you might let me have that forty dollars I paid some fellow or other on account of the programmes for to-night ! "

I do not know if the swindler was ever caught, but in any case it was not until after he had pulled off another piece of work of almost equal simplicity.

A local firm received an order for the hire of a piano to be used at a big charity concert. A few minutes after its installation on the platform, our friend arrived, complete with little black bag.

" I've been ordered to tune the piano for the performance to-night," he said, and no one putting any difficulties in his way, set to work, and in the course of his manipulations managed to break no less than half a dozen hammers. Immediately afterwards he telephoned to the Mayoress of the city, who happened to be the chief organiser of the evening's performance.

" I'm sorry to tell you, Madame," he announced, " that in transporting the piano here they managed to break six hammers. If there's to be any show to-night I guess I'd best go into the city and buy another half-dozen and get busy replacing them."

The lady agreed that under the circumstances that was the only thing to be done.

" Very good, Madame," said the man. " If you'll be good enough to send round thirty dollars and my taxi fare I'll go right away."

Of course the lady sent the money, and equally of course, that was the last they saw of the swindler, though I have always been very curious as to the feelings of the pianist who was called upon to accompany on an instrument with six broken hammers.

Mention of making up my laundry reminds me of the difficulty in our constant travelling of arranging for an adequate supply of clean linen. In this perhaps I was the chief sufferer of the company. Apart from my evening shirts it was a rare occasion when I used less than three collars during a performance; usually my first one was limp with perspiration by the end of the overture.

One good friend to whom I explained the difficulty offered a solution which for a time I thought might fill the bill.

"We have in America," he explained, "collars made of celluloid which at the distance you are from the audience would be quite indistinguishable from the real article. They will neither ruck nor grow limp, and when they're soiled all you have to do is to scrub 'em with an ordinary nailbrush, dry 'em on a hand-towel, and in a couple of minutes there's your clean collars all fine an' dandy."

The idea struck me as excellent. I inspected the collars for sale in the nearest store which supplied them, and I was confident that, as my friend had said, they would pass muster. Hence I bought half a dozen, and from my own point of view found them all that had been claimed for them.

But as occurs so frequently in all branches of the theatrical profession, disillusion, when it came, was provided by the Press. It was at Spokane, Washington, that the morning following our first performance, I opened one of the local papers to read the criticism of our show. The opening sentences were particularly arresting. So far as my memory serves me the dramatic critic began his review as under :

" At 8.15 precisely last night Mr. Theodore Stier, the Musical Director, raised his baton to conduct the overture to the first performance of the Pavlova Session, wearing a celluloid collar of such lustre as to render further illumination of the theatre unnecessary."

Among the charms of one night stands in America was the variety of receptions we met with in some of the smaller cities. One of the most curious experiences we had was in a " hick " or " one-horse " town in Kentucky.

When the train drew up at the station we were met by the Mayor. This was not in itself unusual, but the man himself was very unusual indeed. He was, I think, the most unctuously inquisitive individual it has ever been my fortune to encounter.

There being no conveyance at the station, we were obliged to walk to our hotel, and carry our " grips " into the bargain, which we did to the accompaniment of a crossfire of entirely personal questions from his Worship. And then, after a lull —presumably to take breath—he jerked round to Pavlova.

" Say, marm," he enquired, " do you play cards ? "

" Occasionally," Pavlova said smilingly.

Whereupon, with the swiftness of a heron after

fish, he dived into his pocket, and produced two packs of cards, which he thrust upon the thoroughly mystified Pavlova.

" I sell 'em," he said.

When we got to the hotel, and Pavlova was being shown to her room, he turned to me.

" Say," he demanded huskily, " what does that dame do ? "

" Do ? " I repeated dazedly.

"Sure," he said ; " what does she do ? Sing or act ? "

I explained that while she did neither the one nor the other, she was the world's most famous dancer.

He turned the information over for a moment, and I could see that there was still something upon which he required enlightenment. Eventually it came out.

" She doesn't dance for three hours at a stretch, does she ? " he demanded.

Of the many hundreds of theatres in which we performed throughout the world, one of the most remarkable was the Midway Gardens Theatre in Chicago. There the performance takes place entirely in the open air, a setting I learnt most intensely to dislike. Had the weather been more favourable it is possible that my leanings might be all the other way, because at least this half-cubistic half-Athenian temple has the advantage of seating an exceptionally large audience.

It was in August 1915 that we played there, and although of the thirty-one evenings on no less than twenty-three it poured with rain, even these conditions were insufficient to induce Pavlova to abandon the performances. But with the best will in the world the moment came when she was forced to bow to the inevitable. Apart from the discomfort of the audience and the fact that her make-up was not rainproof, there is no more dangerous experience for a dancer than to perform on a wet stage ; the risk simply wasn't worth while. Speaking for myself I can imagine many more pleasant ways of conducting than under conditions which render it necessary for the librarian of the music to hold an open umbrella over my head.

Even with these drawbacks, however, the fact remains that the Midway Theatre in Chicago is one of the most remarkable in which we were called upon to perform. The National Opera House in Havana may have been more superb, for it is built entirely of white granite in the style of a Venetian Palace ; the tiny Mission Hall in which we were expected to display ourselves in Nashville, Tennessee, where the audience were seated in pews, and Pavlova's dressing-room the organ loft, was more incongruous ; but with one exception the Midway Theatre stands out in my mind as a building which is absolutely unique, even more so than the Imperial Hotel in Tokio, which was designed by the same architect. And in passing it is interesting to recall that while the crowds for " The Dumb Girl of Portici," the only film in which Pavlova ever acted, were taken in Los Angeles, the scenes in which she personally appeared

PAVLOVA FEEDING A BEAR IN YELLOWSTONE PARK

Facing page 104

were shot during the morning in the Midway Gardens at Chicago.

Mention of Tennessee reminds me that not all the romance has yet faded from the Southern and South-westerly States of America. As I shall tell later, there were conditions under which we played in Mexico which were calculated to give rise to apprehension, but not even in that incongruous land do the hotel bell-boys carry out their duties barefooted, and with revolvers sticking most obtrusively from their hip pockets, as was the case in the caravanserai at which we stayed in Waco, Texas.

There is no man of my acquaintance more appreciative of the picturesque than myself, but I think that romance, like whisky, should be diluted before its flavour can really be appreciated. It was under this principle, and to avoid any possible misunderstanding, that in that particular metropolis I made a point of piling every movable article of furniture my bedroom contained against the door each night before retiring, more or less peacefully, to sleep.

What, I wonder, is the exact relationship between dirt and picturesqueness that so often they seem to go hand in hand ? The State of Texas, for instance, is one of the most picturesque in the Union ; it contains also some of the dirtiest theatres in America. Thus, one of my oldest friends was an empty ink bottle which during our first tour I found on the table in my dressing-room in a certain Texan city. A year later, when again

I occupied that same room, my old friend the ink bottle was still there to greet me, and again on the following year and the year after that.

And yet it was in Dallas, Texas, that I came across one of the most beautiful jewellers' shops it has ever been my good fortune to encounter. Here Novikoff, who at that time was Pavlova's partner, purchased a bracelet of three hundred and fifty small pearls of almost unimaginably delicate workmanship, and which resembled more than anything else a piece of Venetian lace. Nor was the price of six hundred and fifty dollars a cent more than it was worth. I happened to be with him when the sale was negotiated, and it was my genuine admiration of its beauty which, eventually, induced Novikoff to buy—a circumstance which the jeweller appeared fully to recognize. Furthermore, his gratitude took practical if surprising form, for at the next town we played in a souvenir of the occasion arrived from him in the form of a pearl tiepin, which must be worth at least twenty pounds.

But however fortunate personally I may have been on that particular tour, the luck did not extend to the company as a whole, and of all the members of it Pavlova herself was the most unfortunate. We commenced at Boston with two separate and distinct misfortunes. The first was that her manager became fired with the ambition to form an opera company in which she would take prominent part ; the combination of the two arts, he argued, would be irresistible.

Sadly against her own better judgment Pavlova was induced to finance the venture, which failed to the extent of a loss of something like a hundred and eighty thousand dollars. And though a considerable proportion of this deficit was retrieved when the company settled down once more to its own regime, the nett result of the tour was distinctly unfortunate.

The second of fate's bludgeonings was in connection with a very handsome Italian singer who recently had joined the company. As is not unusual with men who labour under the dubious blessing of good looks, he considered himself something of a lady-killer. Probably he was; where he made the big mistake was to put his conviction into practice in a city which prides itself more upon its culture than upon the encouragement of chance acquaintanceships in the streets.

I believe she was a very beautiful lady indeed; she was also the wife of the manager of the theatre at which the company was performing !—and when, without the slightest encouragement, our Neapolitan songster endeavoured to what I believe is known as " get off " with her, she displayed no hesitation whatever in making a bid for the purification of public morals by giving the astounded vocalist in charge of the nearest policeman, who promptly marched him off to the station house.

Unfortunately, however, his presence was essential to the performance, and as it is impossible for even an Italian opera singer to be in gaol and on the stage at one and the same time, Pavlova was obliged to appear before the fount of justice to plead for his release.

It was an extraordinary conversation between those two ; Pavlova voluble in English that was more broken than usual on account of her nervousness, the magistrate terse and calmly judicial, but quite obviously succumbing to the influence of such a charming advocate. But, charm or no charm, release the lady-killing Italian he refused definitely to do.

Eventually he was affected by a Solomonic brainwave which I should imagine was far more satisfactory to the respective upholders of their several interests than to the object of their contention. Briefly, the disillusioned Don Juan was permitted to leave the prison under police escort at seven o'clock each evening for the purpose of making his appearance, the escort hovering in the wings within easy striking distance during the whole time their prisoner was warbling impassioned love songs from the stage. Immediately the performance was over, still in charge of two stalwart " cops," the vocalist was marched back to his lonely prison cell. I hesitate to believe that that particular Italian gentleman will ever again practise his hobby in the streets of the most cultured city of America. I should hesitate to believe, also, that he would even recognize it by this particular description.

Speaking of legal proceedings, a still more serious incident occurred at Hamilton, Ontario, in 1910, and one which might have had very serious consequences for the unfortunate person concerned.

At the time Michael Mordkin was Pavlova's partner. In one of our principal items, " The Oriental Ballet," there was a sword dance in which real Turkish scimitars were used, a savage, frenzied affair in which Mordkin used to work himself up to fever heat, whirling his sword about his head with a passion entirely befitting the theme.

And one night the sword broke off at the hilt, the blade whirling over my head to strike the temple of a University student seated in the second row of the stalls.

To prevent an uproar I had no alternative, while the victim was being carried out, but to go on playing as if nothing had happened. Immediately the curtain fell, however, I hurried round to ascertain the exact extent of the damage.

Actually it was very serious ; so much so that it was found necessary to operate in the foyer of the theatre while the performance was still in progress. Of course Mordkin was immediately arrested and held in custody pending the result of the accident. This, as it transpired, was bad enough, for eventually the victim became mentally afflicted. If he had died there is not the slightest doubt that Mordkin would have been charged with manslaughter.

As it was, he was permitted to proceed with the company only on payment of substantial bail. Quite naturally, a suit for damages was entered by the friends of the injured man, with the result —I believe—that Pavlova had to pay twenty thousand dollars in compensation.

But this same Mordkin was always slightly difficult. Pavlova herself is temperamental, as I have mentioned already, but she is an ice-cold stoic compared with Mordkin. Magnificent dancer as undoubtedly he is, there is no denying that he was far from being a tranquillizing influence.

I am inclined to think that his besetting weakness was an undue sensitiveness and a readiness to take offence where a little reflection would have shown that nothing of the kind was intended.

At one time his grievance would be upon the grounds that either on the bills, or on the programmes, Pavlova's name was printed in larger type than his own; at others that she received more attention or consideration from the management.

The most amusing incident in connection with this peculiarity occurred while we were playing at Grand Rapids. After a battle royal over some trivial grievance, and which lasted over many days, I had succeeded at last in effecting a reconciliation between those two temperamental principals And for the rest of that day everything went as harmoniously as experience had taught me it was reasonable to expect.

And then, when to all appearances amity was at its height, the storm renewed itself with a tempestuous violence which made what had gone before seem like an April shower in comparison. Suddenly as we were seated happily at supper, and for no possible reason that any one of us could discover, Mordkin's face began to turn that peculiar shade which with him was the sure forerunner of trouble.

" What is it, Mordkin ? " I enquired in trepidation, but feverishly anxious to keep the peace.

For all the notice he took of me I might not have been included among those present. Instead of replying he picked up the menu and banged it down in front of Pavlova with a violence which caused the table appointments to leap affrightedly in the air, at the same time thrusting his chair back with a force that slid it across the room like a sleigh on ice.

" There you are ! " he shouted, pointing to the menu with a vibrating forefinger. " Now you see ! Frogs legs à la Pavlova ! Always it is yourself ! Never of Mordkin you think, but always Pavlova, Pavlova, Pavlova ! Frogs legs à la Pavlova ! But where is there Frogs Legs à la Mordkin ? Where is anything eatable à la Mordkin ? Tell me that."

Speaking generally we found the American food very much to our taste, particularly as regards the fruit and vegetables.

Was it not that good friend of Great Britain, Ambassador Page, who, when writing to his son from London in the winter before the War, said that the English had only two kinds of vegetables —both cabbage ? And though this is by way of being humorous licence it is none the less a fact that we have much to learn from his countrymen both in the way of the production and preparation of our green-stuffs. With fruit it is a different matter ;

we have no California upon which to draw all the year round.

It was an American, too, I think, who, on his first visit to London, remarked that he knew now why the English drank so much tea—he had tasted their coffee! And speaking by and large it must be admitted that they devote a care and attention to the preparation of coffee which it would be difficult to bring even some of our leading English hotels to appreciate.

I remember one case in particular, which occurred at one of the largest hotels in Baltimore, where the manager took an exceptional pride in his coffee. He was particularly attentive to Pavlóva, and in the course of his good offices urged that we should try his " Café Diable," which, he explained, was made by an Oriental on a special principle of his own.

Eventually, both Pavlova and myself consented to taste this wonderful concoction, with the result that neither of us were able to sleep a wink for the three succeeding nights. Certainly the beverage was delicious to the taste, but its constituents must have included every sleep-dispelling drug in the pharmacopea.

It was at this same hotel, also, where upon arriving home from the theatre one night Pavlova found that the door of her room had been forced, as had also her trunks, that her clothing was distributed all over the room, and every piece of jewellery she had brought with her abstracted. It is probable that had we been staying in the town she might have received compensation from the management. As it was, the loss being but some three hundred pounds in value, it was simply not worth either the time or the money to fight the claim.

Much as both Pavlova and myself appreciated their coffee, there was a beverage we liked still better—the light German-style beer which before the advent of prohibition was such a feature of American life. As, however, this varied in quality according to the district in which it was sold, it came to be an understood thing that in each fresh city we visited I should lose no time in finding out a restaurant with a reputation for dispensing the most palatable brand. After a little experience I discovered that my most reliable informant was likely to be the nearest policeman. What the Force didn't know about beer wasn't worth drinking.

Eventually we arrived in Milwaukee, a city whose population was largely German, the greater proportion of whom were engaged in the manufacture of their national beverage.

The day after our arrival, and in accordance with my usual custom, I approached the traffic cop on duty outside our hotel.

" Excuse me, officer," I said politely, " but can you tell me of any place in Milwaukee where they sell really good German beer ? "

He was a large and opulently-proportioned man of genial eye and generous colouring, and for a moment he regarded me sternly. Then, as though assured that my query was a genuine desire for

H

information, his attitude relaxed. Placing a huge and well-nourished arm about my shoulders in a gesture of comradeship, he waved his other to embrace the whole area of the city.

" Brother," he announced, " there's a place on every block." Adding, reverently, " Thank God ! "

It is a matter of gratification to me that my own relations with the company were always of the happiest possible description. The girls, I think, used to regard me as a kind of adopted uncle— anyway that was the attitude of the great majority of them.

An incident comes to my mind in connection with this of which I never think without amusement. It happened that my birthday fell upon a day when we were travelling to Washington, and that a bevy of journalists boarded the train to interview Pavlova. They broke into the car to interrupt a scene which quite evidently intrigued them more than a little, for I was in the act of being kissed by each one in turn of a queue of extremely pretty and attractive young girls.

" Say," one of the journalists remarked, " it must be some job, being Musical Director to Madame Pavlova ! I guess I'm going out to learn the fiddle."

I assured them with as much earnestness as I could muster that the occasion was exceptional. Those unearned but none the less welcome embraces were tribute only to " Maestro's " birthday, a statement which was greeted by a middle-aged humorist with the announcement that by a curious coincidence he himself was celebrating his majority that very day. Not one of those assembled news-paper men could be brought to believe that to be kissed by practically every member of the company was not part and parcel of the daily routine of a musical conductor. It was not until Pavlova herself dashed tempestuously into the car, threw her arms round my neck, and cried, " Many, Many Happy Returns, *cher ami*," that my reputation as a truth-teller was vindicated.

I have had occasion previously to speak of the respect and affection in which I had every reason to hold those young ladies of the *corps de ballet*. They were in truth a cheery and devoted little company. Their lives were spent in wandering from one hotel to another, rushing from one train to another, playing in one theatre after another. They had little leisure for relaxation. Every single night of the week when they were not performing they were on the train ; more often than not they travelled after the actual performance. Their days were spent rehearsing on the cold boards of dismal and draughty theatres, or practising in the corridors of Pullman cars.

And yet they were never-failingly cheerful ; always up to the scratch in all conditions of work or health or climate. No wonder that Pavlova holds her British girls in such admiration.

As an instance of the hardships which from time to time they are called upon to endure I remember an occasion in Cincinnati, when, owing to the coach in which it was packed having been shunted, the whole baggage of the company failed to arrive. As a consequence every stitch of stage clothing worn by any one of us had to be borrowed And although, speaking for myself, a dress suit loaned by the leader of a local orchestra who happened to be just about twice my own size, together with staring yellow boots, is a fashion which scarcely commends itself as a fitting costume for a musical director, I have to admit that of all the company I was the least inconvenienced by the contretemps. Fortunately, the baggage turned up all right the next day.

CHAPTER VII

THE journey from the States to Mexico is an apparently endless affair of three burning days from El Paso, through countless miles of yellow sand in which there is nothing to relieve monotony but a very occasional and dejected-looking wooden hut, and a few forbidding cactus plants. And once across the border the contrast in customs and ideals of the inhabitants to their neighbours on the American side is striking in the extreme.

But though, like their cousins of the South American republics, the Mexicans are a people who might easily have adopted *manana* (to-morrow) as their national watchword, in matters of public entertainment they have brought punctuality to something resembling a fine art. To be late in raising the curtain at the beginning of a performance or after an interval is an offence which can be wiped out only with—money. Almost I had written that it can be wiped out only with the blood of those responsible. A far-fetched assertion on the face of it, but, as I shall show later, one not without a semblance of justification.

It is a pretty hard life, performing in Mexico. On week days, for instance, we were required to give performances at seven-fifteen and nine-thirty; and on the Sabbath, being the day of rest, an additional show at four o'clock in the afternoon. Above all, it was demanded that we started to the very tick of time, and that precisely fifteen minutes, neither a second more nor less, should be allowed for the intermission.

The penalty for unpunctuality is a fine of fifty dollars, and, judging by the signs, a quick obliteration of the musical director. In any case one Stier more or less would hardly worry a Mexican audience.

To further ensure punctuality it is the custom of the Municipal Comisario to occupy his official seat, watch in hand, and an expression of menace on his face calculated to chill a sterner heart than mine. As a matter of fact we never were late, but from what I could gather in the event of our being so he would have dashed round immediately to the box office and collected the fine of fifty dollars there and then. What would have happened if the takings had not reached that figure I shudder to think.

Our own treatment, however, was exceptionally benevolent. This the Comisario demonstrated when he drew me confidentially aside after the first performance. He was one of the most ruthlessly savage-looking individuals I have ever seen, and at first sight he almost frightened me to death. I found, however, that the extreme truculence of his appearance was almost belied by a more than usually active sense of humour.

" The only times we ever seem likely to be troubled by unpunctuality," he explained, " is in the case of musical comedy companies. On those

OUR PARTY CROSSING INTO MEXICO—AFTER EIGHT MONTHS OF PROHIBITION

Facing page 118

occasions I make a point of going on the stage
and flourishing my largest revolver in the faces of
the principals, and threatening to shoot if there
is a moment's delay in drawing up the curtain.
Of course I haven't the remotest intention of
doing so. But it certainly does ensure promptness."

Personally, however, I was inclined to be a
little dubious as to the entire innocence of his inten-
tions. To me he looked entirely capable of carrying
out his threat; not necessarily to kill, but just for
the fun of the thing and "*pour encourager les
autres.*"

Fortunately, however, there would have been
no need to worry over our financial resources even
should we have been called upon to meet a fine,
for there was no one performance at which we were
not packed to capacity by a house which was
almost embarrassingly enthusiastic.

One curious method employed by various members of the audience to display their approval was
to hurl their huge sombreros on to the stage.
There were times, indeed, when from my seat in
the orchestra the whole air seemed filled with hats.

It was a matter of congratulation to us, however,
to discover that these were not intended to be
kept and worn as headgear by the company.
Speaking personally I am confident they would not
have suited my particular style of beauty, though
I must admit that one or two of the younger girls,
who for fun masqueraded in serapi and sombrero,
looked particularly charming. The idea was that
Pavlova should throw each specimen back to its

owner—a matter of fine discrimination with such a closely packed audience.

So far as I could gather the wealth and social position of a Mexican is shown very much by his headgear, of which he is inordinately proud. As the man of substance thinks little of giving anything from fifty to a hundred dollars for his " party " hat, it is perhaps natural that however demonstrative his artistic enthusiasm, he should take care that at least it is returned to him after it has contributed its quota of praise.

In matters of everyday concern the courtesy of these people is unassailable. I remember once calling in at a drink palace for refreshment on one very hot day, and tendering a silver dollar in payment of the light beer I had ordered. To my surprise the bar-tender politely handed the money back to me. When I asked the reason he explained that one of the habitués of the place, who quite naturally was a total stranger to me, had quietly insisted upon paying for the drink. When I turned to thank my host he bowed with a courtesy which would have done honour to the most punctilious of his Castilian ancestry.

" Señor," he explained gracefully, " the performance of the company of which you are such a distinguished member has given everyone in this saloon such unexampled happiness that we count it a great honour you should consent to drink with us."

In writing of this universal courtesy, however, I find it necessary to make a mental reservation as regards the Mexican Musical Union. If the sister organisation in America was autocratic, they themselves constituted an unlimited monarchy whose word was law. Nor were they conspicuous by any childlike trust in the fundamental honesty of human nature, a lack of faith quite clearly demonstrated by the fact that instead of drawing their salary weekly, the orchestra insisted upon payment each night.

Furthermore, if by some mischance the money should happen not to have been forthcoming by the end of the first act, they would most politely but resolutely have declined to permit the curtain to rise for the second.

While on the subject of payment I should imagine that the Mexican cashier is selected as much for his muscular development as for his abilities as an accountant. To be a paymaster there is a man-sized job. Happening to have some business in front of the house one evening, I encountered there a stalwart who was staggering under the weight of a sack about the size of the average coal bag of commerce. Curiosity aroused, I enquired both as to his business and his burden. He informed me that he was on his way to pay the orchestra their nightly emolument, and that by the time this was accomplished the sack would be empty. The explanation is contained in the fact of there being no paper currency in Mexico.

One of the most interesting and arresting features of the national life is the veneration which everywhere is shown for the memory of Cervantes. One eloquent demonstration of this is the monument erected to that immortal in Chapultepec Park, and a very unique and eloquent memorial it is. The work is executed in blue and white tiles, upon each one of which is depicted an episode from the story of Don Quixote. Surrounding the monument are benches, and, extraordinary to relate, book-shelves, upon which are copies of the book intended for the use of those who take their pleasure in the Park. There can be no greater tribute to the sincerity of the honour in which Cervantes is held than the one significant fact that in a country which not even its most enthusiastic protagonist could acclaim for meticulous honesty, not one of these volumes has ever been known to be stolen.

Always I have held it as a misfortune that the late Sir W. S. Gilbert was a stranger to Mexico. There is so much there in which he would have found delight, and which his genius could have turned to account. Though in entirely different directions, Mexico is as much a country of con-tradictions as is the greater republic across its borders.

For instance, there is in Mexico City an extremely ancient and interesting survival of long dead civilisation in the form of an Aztec temple, which has a wholly unexpected annex of an underground crypt which, with a practicality I failed to observe in other and possibly more urgent directions, the powers that were had transformed into one of the finest and most elaborately equipped drinking bars I have ever visited.

One of the most interesting buildings in which I conducted was the Bull Ring in the same city, a venue in which it is possible that to take a " steer's " life is the Alpha and Omega of its purpose may have contributed no little to my own efficiency.

The reason of our appearance there was that it was represented to us that the prices it was necessary to charge in the Opera House were entirely prohibitive to the poorer classes, and that as these were quite as artistically enthusiastic as their richer brethren, considerable dissatisfaction had resulted. It was to meet this demand, then, that Pavlova arranged for two performances in the Bull Ring. And although that open-air arena is considerably more than twice the size of the Albert Hall, it was literally packed to capacity upon each occasion.

And at the second performance it rained.

Pavlova carried on as well and for as long as it remained possible to do so. Longer, in fact, than was safe—already I have explained the real danger of dancing on a wet stage. In addition to that her make-up, and that of every one on the stage, was streaming down in rivulets. For the sake of all concerned it was absolutely necessary to ring down the curtain after the performance had lasted only a very short time indeed.

And then there was trouble with a capital T. Neither explanation nor expressions of regret were of the slightest avail.

Small, comparatively, as they were, the prices

paid for admission represented a greater sacrifice to the audience than easily can be understood by those who have not been brought into contact with the poverty of the Mexican lower classes. In comparison with the loss of the performance a rainstorm meant nothing at all. All that concerned the audience was to see that they got their money's worth.

To continue the performance was impossible; to satisfy the house that this was so a greater impossibility still. Eventually it was represented to us by the management, and in no uncertain terms either, that the stage door still stood where it did, and that if we were wise we should employ that exit while the going remained good.

Which we did.

One of the difficulties experienced by Pavlova in Mexico City, and which to a greater or lesser extent was shared by the whole company, was the altitude at which it is situated—seven thousand five hundred feet above sea level. It was only to be expected that the rarity of the atmosphere rendered breathing under the strenuous conditions of dancing extremely difficult, and the consequent strain on her heart threatened at one time to be serious. Thus we were not sorry when the time came for us to leave.

There is quite a large British colony in Mexico City with an English Club where we received a hearty welcome and great hospitality. One of the cheeriest members, and who was extremely popular and in great demand by Pavlova's Company—from whom, incidentally, as with all artists, he refused to accept any fee for professional services—was Dr. Cockrell.

An Englishman, he had been in Mexico for forty years, and at the time of our visit had retired from practice. In spite of this, however, and with the same kindness of heart which had impelled him to build a hospital at which patients receive free treatment, he held himself still at the disposal of anyone who made a bid for his services.

In a climate so removed from any to which we had been accustomed, it is not a matter of surprise that some few of the company should have been affected by minor ailments, nor that the patients should have preferred to be treated by one of their own nationality.

And let me say at once that Dr. Cockrell is the only practitioner within my experience whose medicines were as universally popular as he was himself. Indeed, it was some little time before I ceased to wonder at the avidity with which the afflicted disposed of their draughts. My surprise, however, lessened considerably when I discovered that each dose of medicine administered by this most understanding of physicians was camouflaged benevolently in the form of a cocktail.

We travelled from Mexico back to New York by boat, a journey which all appeared very much to enjoy. *En route* our boat called at the apparently unimportant city of Progreso, Yucatan.

It was such an unimpressive-looking place, indeed, that we none of us could make out the reason for our stopping there; certainly it was neither to load nor to discharge cargo—not, at least, any of strictly mercantile description. And then, quite suddenly, the mystery was enhanced by a comparatively large influx of fresh passengers. Nor were these Mexicans; on the contrary, they were as charming a group of American girls as ever it has been my good fortune to encounter. All were young and quite obviously in the highest possible spirits. What, I wondered, had they been doing in such a desolate spot as the inaptly named Progreso?

It was the purser, eventually, who "put me wise."

In the State of Yucatan divorce was obtained more quickly and easily than in almost any part of the world, and from the American point of view possessed the additional advantage that a dissolution granted there was recognised by the United States Courts. Each of our new passengers, then, was an American wife whose sojourn there had been for the purpose of taking advantage of this broad-minded enactment, and, the divorce having been granted, was returning, unshackled by domesticity, to her native land. Hence the high spirits which kept the rest of the passengers on tip-toes during the remainder of our voyage to New York.

After so long in the United States and Mexico it was a change to cross the American border into Canada.

Almost immediately upon our arrival at Montreal we were honoured by a gala performance which was attended by the Duke of Connaught—who at that time was Governor-General of Canada—and his suite.

Upon being notified of His Royal Highness's intention my first thought, of course, was that it would be necessary to play the British National Anthem. To my surprise I could discover no copy of " God Save the King " included in the music belonging to the theatre. The American-Italians who constituted the personnel of the orchestra had never even heard of it.

My astonishment was still greater when I found that it was impossible to obtain the orchestral parts anywhere in the entire city of Montreal. Since the War, which contributed so greatly to strengthen the links between the Mother Country and Canada, I have no doubt that state of affairs has become remedied. Even prior to 1914 the Province of Quebec was perhaps the only one in the Dominion suffering from this dearth; it must be remembered how predominantly French is that part of the North American Continent.

Eventually I solved the difficulty by employing Weber's Jubilee Overture, a German patriotic tune, the last sixteen bars of which are identical with the British National Anthem.

The performance was received with great enthusiasm, and was in all respects a brilliant success. After the fall of the final curtain Pavlova was notified that the Royal party would come behind the scenes to tender His Royal Highness's personal congratulations.

Although Pavlova was delighted at the honour

to be conferred upon her, the position was one of some slight embarrassment. The circumstance that we were leaving Montreal that same night did not leave us an undue amount of time to pack and reach the station. Hence it was necessary to commence moving the scenery and effects the moment the curtain dropped.

Actually Pavlova kept the Royal party waiting quite an appreciable time before making her appearance, though, with the understanding with which the Duke is so identified, this was the cause of no embarrassment, and necessarily short as was the interview it remains one of Pavlova's happiest memories; one, in addition, to which there was a quite amusing sequel. For when in due time we were safely installed in the train, it was to discover that Pavlova's little dog Teddy, to which she was greatly attached, was not included among those present on the station.

There was, then, nothing for it but that I dash hastily back to the theatre in search of the missing favourite.

In vain I peered into every corner of the pitch-dark stage and dressing-rooms. At last I was compelled to return and report my lack of success to Pavlova.

Quite naturally she was greatly distressed, particularly as there was a Russian girl attendant whose personal job it was to look after Teddy and see that no harm came to him. Pavlova sent for the girl, and in no measured terms gave her precise opinion of her carelessness. Goaded by a manifest sense of injustice the culprit very hotly resented the charge.

"If you *will* have strangers behind the stage," she contended, "then I must refuse to accept responsibility for anything that is missing!"

Surely this must be the only time His Royal Highness the Duke of Connaught has been suspected of dog stealing!

Writing of Teddy brings to my mind an incident which occurred in Montgomery, Alabama.

Pavlova and I were taking the little dog out for an airing. Missing him from our side for a moment, we turned to see him being made much of by a man who, quite obviously, was very much of a dog-lover. Indeed, his fancy was so evident that I turned back—just in case. He looked up.

"Say, this is a fine dog, all right," he said enthusiastically.

I agreed with him that Teddy was, indeed, a very nice dog.

"Say, I should like to buy this here dog," the stranger went on, and made a gesture to indicate Pavlova. "Do you think the woman would sell him?" he enquired.

I replied that I was perfectly sure that "the woman" would not for a moment contemplate doing so, a reply which appeared both to surprise and annoy him.

"But I must *have* him!" he proclaimed. "Just tell her that—I must have him."

"But, my dear sir," I protested, "you *can't* have

I

him. The lady is very fond of the dog, and absolutely refuses to part with him."

With that he turned dejectedly and protestingly away, and followed by Teddy, Pavlova and I continued in the opposite direction.

We had not progressed many yards, however, before we were brought to a stop by a shout of " Hi ! "

We turned, and found that twenty yards down the street the canine enthusiast, too, had stopped.

" Hi, mister ! " he shouted.

" What is it ? " I shouted back.

" Tell the girl," he yelled, " that if only she'll let me have the dog—I'll marry her ! "

Another episode which had a dog for its motif occurred at Monte Catini—the same place, it will be remembered, where Pavlova so summarily dealt with the two ladies who, in order to gain her acquaintance, endeavoured to force their way into her box at the theatre.

We were out walking with the dog, when, without a word of warning a policeman lassoed that outraged animal, and then intimated that we were to accompany him to the police station.

Arrived there we were faced by a stout and extremely unemotional Commissary of Police, for whose benefit Pavlova produced one of the finest oratorical efforts of her career. With extreme wealth of detail she proclaimed her sense of outrage at what, without the slightest explanation on the part of the officer responsible—as it was without the slightest knowledge on our part of having been guilty of any breach of the law—amounted practically to arrest in the open street.

She pointed out that Monte Catini was dependent very largely upon visitors for its prosperity, and that for distinguished foreigners to be treated in such high-handed fashion was an extremely bad advertisement for its attraction.

She said many other things besides, all equally eloquent and convincing. It was not until she had been speaking for a full ten minutes, and without the least response from the Commissary, that it dawned upon her that he had not understood a single word of what she had been saying.

Not to be daunted, Pavlova started to say it all over again, though as this time she spoke in Italian, of which her mastery was not exact, this second effort was by no means so convincing as the first. And all the time of her oratory the Commissary, without once looking up, was writing industriously in a book.

When the flow ceased he waited an appreciable moment to make certain that this, at last, was the end. Reassured, apparently, by the comparative silence, he looked up.

" Ten lira," he said simply.

And before we were allowed to take the dog or ourselves from the custody of the police station, ten lira it was.

It transpired that without any knowledge of the regulations which forbade it, we had allowed a dog in the streets without a muzzle.

Pavlova's love for everything British was never

more clearly demonstrated than upon her first day in Montreal. It was the policemen, in a uniform identical with that of their English comrades, which especially aroused her enthusiasm.

"Do you not think I might embrace one of those English bobbies?" she demanded of me with sparkling eyes.

I told her that a traffic block at that hour of the day would be a very serious matter indeed. She compromised by insisting upon shaking hands with two young and highly embarrassed members of the constabulary.

Actually our progress through Canada was one long-drawn-out triumph. In the City of Quebec Pavlova was "presented" with a golden key of the city by the Mayor. Actually it was necessary to take the will for the deed, the key being twelve feet long and held, not without some muscular strain, by two stalwart policemen. Nevertheless it seemed to me a charming custom, this symbol of welcome to a distinguished visitor.

After the ceremony was completed the Fire Brigade was called out, and with Pavlova seated next to the driver on one of the engines, and led by the Mayor and other officials, an informal processional drive was taken through what undoubtedly is the most picturesque city in Canada.

Vancouver was another city which gave us a glorious welcome, not only at the theatre, but elsewhere.

After the performance one night I remember us going into supper at one of the large restaurants,

PAVLOVA'S JOY AT SEEING BRITISH POLICEMEN IN CANADA AFTER LONG ABSENCE FROM BRITISH SOIL

Facing page 132

only to find it packed to the doors by people in evening dress who had come in after our performance. As we appeared everyone in the room stood up, and this attracting the attention of the manager he came quickly forward to greet us. And then, as the room was absolutely full, he had a table and chairs brought in and a space cleared for us to sup comfortably.

Accustomed to arousing attention Pavlova ate her meal quite undisturbed by the prevailing interest. Suddenly, however, came a loud knocking on one of the near-by tables, designed to bring the room to attention.

It was an Englishman who spoke. On the ground of the universal interest in Pavlova's presence and the common desire to pay her tribute he excused himself for addressing a company the majority of which were strangers to him. He spoke of the honour the great dancer had done Vancouver in appearing in the city, and of the great influence which, by her art, she exercised throughout the world. He concluded by requesting the band to play the Russian National Anthem—the incident, of course, took place prior to the revolution in that country.

Of the many tributes which have been paid to Pavlova during our world tours this is among her most pleasant memories.

CHAPTER VIII

PAVLOVA is in the habit of describing the time she spent in Japan as one of the most inspiring in her career. I should like to add a personal rider to the effect that it was also the most interesting, and this in spite of the supreme difficulties I encountered in my duties as musical director.

My main trouble, of course, was to obtain adequate orchestras, a difficulty which after only a little experience I came to regard as insurmountable. Great an admirer as I am of the Japanese in general, in frankness I am obliged to confess that tribute does not extend to an enthusiasm for their orchestral music, which to my mind and that of the company was terrible in the extreme.

In Tokio particularly was this the case, because the theatre there being an Imperial one it was against every tenet of national etiquette to hurt their feelings by showing dissatisfaction. And they went on, and on, and on! In Tokio, as everywhere else, their politeness was as remarkable as their patience was unshakable and their endurance inexhaustible. On my arrival the first morning they were awaiting me, and at the moment of my appearance rose from their seats, and then, as if impelled by a single impulse, all bowed very low

from the waist. It was only during the rehearsal
that I discovered it took them no less than four
hours to go through the overture to Schubert's
"Rosamunde," which is composed to occupy seven
minutes. Nothing dismayed and entirely undis-
couraged, these gracious enthusiasts stuck to their
job with the grim and quiet persistency of mosquitoes.

But difficulties, they say, occur only to be sur-
mounted, and at last even this handicap was
overcome.

By a stroke of good fortune for which I devoutly
thanked the gods, it came to my knowledge that
playing in a café in Soerabaya, Java, were three
Russian musicians : a violinist, pianist, and 'cellist,
each of whom was a medallist at the Imperial Con-
servatory of Moscow.

Without a moment's delay we wired these
gentlemen, offering them positions in Pavlova's
orchestra—I did not think it necessary to mention
that to all intents and purposes they were to *be* the
orchestra.

Flattered, apparently, at such distinguished recognition of their abilities, they were almost as prompt
in their acceptance of the offer as we had been in
making it. Thus I knew that the greater portion
of my travail was overcome.

From the first I was greatly impressed with
the extraordinary zest displayed by all classes of
Japanese for the adequate understanding of a
form of art which is so entirely remote from any of
their own. That Pavlova succeeded in evoking

spontaneous appreciation for her work is sufficiently
evidenced by an occasion in Tokio when at the
end of " The Dying Swan," to our astonishment
a very exalted and dignified official appeared on
the stage, and after having presented Pavlova with
a gold medal, delivered a speech, which I make
no apology for reproducing.

" Madame Anna Pavlova," he declaimed, " your
name as the most distinguished in the realm of the
Russian Ballet has been well known here. It is
quite natural, therefore, that the nation whose love
of art is of no small degree should have impatiently
awaited your arrival here since the first news was
received of your proposed visit to these shores.
The fact that the audience at the Imperial Theatre
unanimously shower words of admiration is an
eloquent testimonial to the exquisiteness and adapt-
ness of your performance. We have now decided,
Madame, to present you with our medal, which
is to be given to those most prominent in any kind
of art, in order to give expression to our high sense
of gratitude for your visit here from afar and the
contribution you have made to our art, as we
believe the nation's high respect and affection for
you is actuated by the same spirit."

The Imperial Theatre in Tokio is in every way
exceptional from those in any of the other ten
Japanese cities in which we played ; as the capital
it has the only modern theatre, complete with seating
accommodation and stage equipment in Japan ; as
a matter of fact it is very similar to His Majesty's
Theatre in London. Until one became used to the

conditions, those other theatres were somewhat disconcerting. Strictly speaking there is no seating accommodation at all, the audiences—in which, Tokio and Yokohama apart, there was not one white face included—the entire audience either sat or knelt on the ground in a kind of shallow frame about four inches high, in one corner of which was a small box, filled apparently with sand, but underneath a burning charcoal designed for lighting the chain of cigarettes every individual spectator consumes during the performance. Also, I found it disconcerting at first to be expected to carry on my conducting with a swarm of children climbing on and all over the stage—even to the very feet of Pavlova as she danced. Equally disconcerting was it to see their small heads poked round the doors of the dressing-rooms when we were changing. There is nothing knowingly impolite or mischievous in this; merely is it a naive curiosity which it is impossible to resent.

Writing of dressing-rooms reminds me that these were not the least of our professional trials, as the hotel accommodation was not the least of our private ones.

Apart from the Imperial Hotel, Tokio—an Alice in Wonderland caravanserai to which I shall refer later—in neither hotel bedroom nor theatre dressing-room was there any furniture of any description, if I except a small curved wooden block in the sleeping apartment upon which ladies are supposed to rest their heads while asleep, in order not to disarrange their elaborately dressed coiffure. Otherwise there are no dressing-tables, no carpet, no chairs, no wardrobes—in the case of a bedroom just what at first I mistook for a grass mat rolled up and propped into a corner. This, it was explained, was sheets, blankets, pillows, and bedstead combined. Not until then was I able to realise how easy in the East it must have been to obey the command: "Take up thy bed and walk." And incidentally, and from personal experience, I have no hesitation in declaring that so far as Japan is concerned it is far easier to walk with a bed than to sleep in it.

Strictly speaking the walls of these rooms are not walls at all, only paper screens through which rather embarrassingly it was impossible not to hear everything that went on in the adjoining apartment. I remember one night occupying the next room to Pavlova, and neither of us being able to sleep (which considering the accommodation was not altogether to be wondered at), pushing my finger through the wall to enable us to carry on a conversation.

If my memory serves me correctly it was the very next morning that she knocked at the door of my room to enquire the whereabouts of the bathroom. As I had no more idea of this than she had, we set off together to look for it, and by dint of enquiries conducted by signs, a certain door was pointed out to us. Under the impression that this led to a corridor from which the bathrooms abutted, we had no hesitation in opening it—and still less in closing it again.

We had enquired for the bathroom, and we had found it in full measure and brimming over. It was the most generously proportioned apartment of its kind I ever saw; designed not for one ablutionist, but for fifteen or twenty at a time—and of both sexes. At the time of our very brief inspection the room, like the landlady in the " Cuckoo in the Nest," was " fully occupied."

There is, however, no suggestion of immorality in this communal bathing. To the Japanese it is as natural for men and women to share a bath as it is for us to share a table at meals. Nudity is simply not noticed—a disregard which is apt to be slightly embarrassing. The weather was very hot during our visit, and the scene shifters perspired very freely. Installed at the back of the stage were several shower baths, which in consequence of the prevailing heat were very freely used during the performance—with the ladies of the ballet passing continually to and fro from the dressing-rooms !

Man is an adaptable creature, however, and we were old campaigners, so that it was not long before we became accustomed even to the unusual conditions of Japanese hotels. There was one town, indeed, Hiroshima, where we would have been glad to take up our quarters in those bare rooms which at first had appeared so entirely lacking in comfort. But in the whole town was no hotel of any description.

There was nothing for it, then, but for the whole company to sleep in the dressing-rooms of the theatre. Of all the nights of our world tours, perhaps, these were the most uncomfortable.

It was not so much that we were obliged to sleep on the floor ; we had become accustomed to that. It was not so much that there was nowhere to hang our clothes, or a place where we could wash ; those conditions also we had become resigned to. What worried us in particular were the visitors, which, the moment we lay down and quiet reigned, began to invade our quarters. I did not know there was so large a variety of the insect world : beetles, cockroaches, spiders, and innumerable other specimens of multi-legged crawlers that would have given nightmare to an entymologist. And with the coming of dark the rooms were infested with enormous bats, which swooping here and there added considerably both to our discomfort and the prevailing eerieness.

It was then that Algeranoff, the youngest and boldest member of the company, a fair-haired English boy of quite unusual talent, especially distinguished himself. He it was who constituted himself executioner-in-chief, and I am afraid obtained more work than rest. Innumerable times in the nightmare hours of those few nights was he summoned by feminine shrieks from the adjoining dressing-rooms ; innumerable times he went forth, slipper in hand, and at the behest of that clamour put to death some new and foul invader. For that period at least Algeranoff was by far the most popular member of the company.

Contrast, then, these quarters with those we

occupied at the Imperial Hotel at Tokio, the architect of which was that same American, Wright,
who was responsible for the Midway Gardens
Theatre in Chicago. Whether this Japanese effort
was by way of being a joke I was never able to
decide ; if it was designed to test the adaptability
and ingenuity of the guests was equally uncertain.
In any case the Cubistic spirit of its decorations
was extended, also, to its conveniences.

The staircase was of stone, but as full of holes
as a Gruyère cheese. There was electric lighting in
all the rooms, the switches out of reach, the brackets
so placed as to be of the least possible use to the
occupants. One day the telephone rang in my
bedroom. When I looked about for the instrument
it was nowhere to be seen.

However, the bell rang and rang, and I looked
and looked. The more it rang, the more persistently
I searched, and the more I searched the more it
rang. Then it occurred to me that for a telephone
the sound appeared to come from rather high up.
The only piece of furniture in the room of an altitude
to correspond with the origin of the sound was the
wardrobe. So placing a chair beside it I groped
on the top. All I could discover was a square box,
which, more from curiosity than hope, I opened.
And here, ensconced shyly within, was the instrument.

It was this same telephone through which was
transmitted one of the most baffling conversations
of my experience. When the bell rang the sole
response I was able to obtain to my reply was

what to all seeming was an echo of myself. Hence, as it was an hotel call, I went downstairs with the idea of finding out who was having a little game with me, and discovered that my cross-talk conversationalist was none other than the local secretary of the Young Men's Christian Association. Complete with expression of annoyance I approached him.

"Mr. Stier ? " he said genially.

"For the twentieth time—*yes*," I said. "I *am* Mr. Stier. Who are you ? "

"Mr. Stier," he repeated genially.

"Yes," I said, "I am Mr. Stier. Get that firmly fixed into your mind. *I—am—Mr.—Stier.* And now, what about you returning confidence for confidence by telling me your own name ? "

"Mr. Stier," he repeated amiably. "That's what I've come to tell you."

By this time I was debating whether the man was a joke or merely an imbecile. I was inclined rather towards the latter. I said, as patiently as I was able :

"Once more, *what* is it that you have come to tell me ? " Adding : "And for your information, I am *still* Mr. Stier ! "

He nodded.

"I know," he said. "So am I. My name is Stier also."

For some reason this annoyed me more than ever.

"Then why in the world didn't you say so," I hotly demanded.

Perhaps not unreasonably the gentleman looked rather hurt.

"But I've been telling you so for the last ten minutes," he protested, "and all you did was to go on repeating my name."

"But it was *you* who kept on repeating mine," I contended.

He half turned away.

"Well, anyway," he said, "you've satisfied me that you're not my brother Theodore, and that's all I came to find out."

By this time I had begun to realise that I must have appeared to him as great an ass as, indubitably, he had seemed to me. I felt it was up to me to make what amends I could.

"I hope your brother Theodore has a better temper than this one," I said.

The advance could not have been better received, nor the response more adequate.

"I don't know about temper," he said, "but though he happens to be a musician, I doubt very much if he could have reached your position."

Although much of what I have written of Japan may appear rather to negative the note of enthusiasm with which I commenced this chapter, the inconveniences I have mentioned were negligible in comparison with the very real happiness we found in other directions. In no country in which we travelled were we received with such wholehearted kindness as was the case in Japan. In this I am not speaking so much of the enthusiasm displayed for our performances, as of the consideration and hospitality which everywhere, and from all classes, was accorded us. Nothing which could add to our pleasure or that went to honour Pavlova was too much for this wonderful people.

Their great joy was to take us to see any and every type of Japanese entertainment One of these which stands out prominently in my memory was a shamisen party at the house of Hiraska, the famous Japanese artist, who for our entertainment staged a blood-curdling drama based on the old legend of " Susanov and the Serpent."

The room in which the play took place was as unusual as it was beautiful. In the middle of the apartment was an oval-shaped flower-bed blooming with many kinds of Japanese blossom, and it was at the borders of this bed that supper was served, while the performance was taking place. Beside each guest, also, was placed a present consisting of some small example of Japanese art; Pavlova's was a very beautifully embroidered silk kimono, my own a silk embroidered cigarette-case.

From a Western point of view the play itself was as unusual as the setting in which it was performed. So far as I was able to follow the plot, it appeared that the serpent from which the drama takes part of its title had eaten seven of the king's daughters, having accomplished which, not unnaturally he found it necessary to pause for breath and the absorption of liquid before coming to the dessert, which was to consist of the eighth and sole surviving member of the family.

Susanov, the king, who had witnessed the mastica-

PAVLOVA ENTERTAINED BY THE STAFF OF AN ENGLISH PAPER RUN ENTIRELY BY JAPANESE

Facing page 144

tion of his family with a detached and academic interest which spoke volumes for his sense of hospitality, called for a bowl of saki for the refreshment of his guest, and then sat waiting patiently for the consequent intoxication. Then, satisfied apparently that his duties of host had been adequately fulfilled, he resumed his vigil until such time as, having slept it off, the serpent would be ready for the next and final course. That was all.

The audience accepted this with complete seriousness. To me, however, the interest was more academic. Truly is Japan a country where, despite the wave of modernism which of late years has elevated her to such a predominant position in the East, tradition dies hard. This play was enacted exactly as would have been the case in England before the Reformation. All the players were men, and all were masked.

Perhaps one of the reasons why I was so carefree at this time was that I had landed in the country immediately upon the heels of one of the most arduous tasks which up to that time I had been called upon to perform.

Immediately before our embarkation in England it was discovered that all three of our trunks of music had disappeared " without trace." A more serious loss could not well have occurred, for it was one which could be replaced only with the utmost difficulty. A large proportion of the music was in manuscript, duplicates of which could be obtained only in Russia.

K

So while M. Dandré hurried abroad to replace as much as possible, that which we had been successful in obtaining in England had all to be rearranged. The residue I had no option but to re-write from memory, and because so much of what was lost would be required immediately, it was necessary for me to give not less than eighteen hours a day to the work.

All the way out to Quebec on the *Empress of France*, and in a heat quite unusual for the Atlantic passage, I was kept hard at it, and again from Vancouver to Japan on the *Empress of Canada*. Hence my joy and relief to discover on reaching Yokohama that I had completed two entire programmes, and thus was able to give myself up to the unrestrained enjoyment of this old land; to revel in the rich colours of the picturesque scenes, the sight of porters in their vivid mauve and brown gowns and pointed straw hats, of children waving flags bearing the inscription in Japanese, " Welcome to Pavlova," and of the less æsthetic joys of press representatives demanding interviews and photographs.

It is possible, however, that my pleasure would have been slightly damped if I had known then what some little time later came to my knowledge —that all the missing trunks concerning which I had lost so much sleep were lying securely in Pavlova's house at Hampstead.

One of the first places we visited after arriving in Tokio was the famous gardens, Kagetsu-an-Tusrumi, a pleasure ground something reminiscent of a cross between the Zoological Gardens and the White City at Shepherd's Bush.

On that occasion our hosts were the members of a Ladies' Club, who jointly and severally set themselves to see that we were shown, and enjoyed, every amenity the Gardens provided. What personally appealed to me most, however, was a large notice, printed in English, displayed prominently outside the enclosure which was set aside for dancing, and of which the following is an exact copy :

NO CHEEK-TO-CHEEK DANCING.

NO SHIMMYING OR SHAKING.

I found it difficult to accustom myself to the Japanese attitude towards women in general. The first two or three times we were guests in a Japanese household the absence of a hostess was rather a matter of wonder, especially as, on looking up, I would discover the wife of our host standing in a corner with the servants.

The diet, too, was a matter of some difficulty, though it is only fair to say that as soon as this was realised our various hosts lost no time in providing food of a kind more palatable to Western guests.

So far as I could gather, the Japanese themselves live chiefly on nearly raw fish, together with rice and pickles eaten from a little square box. I do not quite know when, or how, the ladies of a Japanese household take their meals, though judging by what I observed in the dining-cars of trains, these must be rather impromptu affairs. I noticed then that the gentlemen helped themselves to repletion from each dish, the small quantity of food remaining at the bottom of each being the portion reserved for the female members of the family. And though the ladies did not appear to resent this in the least, I found it impossible to rid myself of a feeling of acute discomfort at the custom.

I found it equally uncomfortable, also, to be obliged to take off my shoes every time I crossed the threshold of a Japanese house or shop. In the first place it entailed a lot of what I felt to be unnecessary trouble, and in the next, being a bachelor, and always on the move at that, I was never altogether prepared to guarantee the entire soundness of my hosiery. And I defy anyone to retain the requisite poise and dignity when confronted with one's own big toe staring coyly up from a large hole in the foot of one's sock !

Nevertheless there is no getting away from the custom. Even in the big departmental stores no exception is made to the universal rule. As one approaches the door it is to be pounced upon by a porter, guardian over a pile of slippers which for any assurance one has to the contrary may have been used by all the coolies in the city. This official refuses to allow you to enter the store until your own footwear is replaced by a pair from his stock, or, alternatively, canvas overshoes. Hence, if one is wise, or at any rate particular, one carries one's own slippers.

It was in the purchase of my own pair of these

that I encountered an example of the extraordinary courtesy which prevails everywhere in Japan. It was quite a small shop, and when I entered, the proprietor was nursing a tiny baby. When I had made known what I wanted, he regretted that slippers were not included among his stock, but endeavoured to explain exactly where they could be purchased. As, however, his English was as unintelligible to me as my Japanese was to him, we did not get very far.

To his Japanese mind, then, remained only one thing to be done. He called his wife, and to her handed over the baby. Then, as if it was the most natural procedure in the world, he conducted me a good mile and a half until the shop of his recommendation was reached. There he bowed, and left me. It would be a somewhat exceptional shopkeeper who, in Europe, and for the benefit of an entire stranger, would put himself to a similar amount of trouble, I'm thinking.

One of the most brilliant sights within my memory was a ceremony, known as the " Jidaematuri," which, on October 27th of each year, takes place in Kyoto, in honour of Kuramu, the founder of the city. We were taken there by the proprietor of our hotel, who, ninety minutes after he had greeted us in full native costume, turned up to act as our escort in a suit that quite obviously had been made in New York.

The pageant, which is designed to illustrate the history of the town for the last thousand years, is taken so seriously that a law has been passed compelling every inhabitant of the city to take part in it at least once every five years.

It was a most impressive sight, to which realism was lent by the fact that the groups representing each period were dressed, not in replicas, but in the actual costumes worn by their ancestors at the time depicted. Additional interest, too, was in the comments and conversation of our host, who was conversant with the history of the town and its customs with a minuteness which would have surprised me more had I not already been enabled to realise the wonderful civic pride and national patriotism with which every one of his countrymen is affected.

CHAPTER IX

IT was in Tokio that we were honoured with the presence of royalty at our performance, in the person of Prince Kuni, brother-in-law of the Crown Prince.

When the word came round for Pavlova to proceed to the Royal box for presentation, for the first time in my experience I was included in the command.

On reaching the box, however, I quickly discovered the reason for the compliment. The Prince's equerry was the Marquis Tokugavw, and he it was who had requested that I might be sent for. So while his Royal master was chatting with Pavlova, the Marquis entered into a discussion with me on the subject of European music, of which he was a great enthusiast, as he was regarding England and English customs, a *penchant* of which his evening clothes, palpably of Bond Street origin, was my first indication. He had spent five years in Cambridge, and during that time it was his delight to go up to London each Sunday for the Queen's Hall concerts. During the conversation he asked me if I thought Pavlova would accept an invitation to a reception at his house. On my replying that I was quite sure she would be delighted, he promised to lose no time in making the necessary arrangements.

In due time the invitation came. The reception was held in his very beautiful grounds, and was attended principally by Europeans, most of the guests being from the various Embassies. I was rather intrigued to notice, moreover, that these grounds contained not one house, but two ; one on the Japanese plan, as a concession to national susceptibilities, the other, and in which he spent the greater portion of his time, entirely of English design and furnishing.

After the proceedings had lasted about an hour he drew me aside.

" Let us slip away by our two selves for a few minutes," he said. " I should like to show you my music room."

And the first thing I saw as I passed through the door was a large signed photograph of Sir Henry J. Wood, with whom I was delighted to discover that my host had made fast friends during his sojourn in England. There and then we sat down and indited a joint postcard to our mutual and eminent acquaintance.

Besides two beautiful Steinway pianos there was, in the room, a large range of bookshelves filled to capacity with volumes, the majority of these larger than those one is accustomed to see in a library devoted entirely to literature. When I commented upon this, my host explained that the volumes contained nothing but music.

" I am very proud of my musical library," he said. " So much so, indeed, that I am prepared to challenge you to think of any orchestral score that is not included on those shelves."

I mentioned one casually, and he shrugged his shoulders.

" Please, Mr. Stier," he said deprecatingly, " think of one which is not in quite such universal possession."

Rather intrigued by his attitude, I set myself to think of the composer least likely to be represented in his collection. Finally, I decided upon a particularly obscure work by Balakireff.

Within a couple of minutes, by the aid of a pair of steps, he brought down a volume from one of the higher shelves, and without hesitation produced the score.

That pleasant visit occurred quite a few years ago, but there has been no Christmas since when the Marquis and I have not exchanged greetings.

The more I travelled through the country the more I was impressed at the extreme ardour displayed everywhere for Western literature. In almost every city we visited it was a common sight to see the students reading as they walked along the street. More than once I took the trouble to ascertain the name of the author with whom they were so engaged. In each case the book was a European or American classic.

To a man, these students were enthusiastic devotees of George Bernard Shaw, of whose works and philosophy they had a knowledge as extensive as it was profound. Other authors in demand were Maupassant, Schnitzler, Hauptmann, and Nietzsche.

Unless I am mistaken Japan is destined within the next fifty years to take a prominent place in the hierarchy of literature.

I remember Pavlova being invited to a reception by the proprietor of a Japanese newspaper that was printed entirely in English; I recollect, too, my surprise on being told that there was no single worker of European nationality on the staff. The paper was written, edited, printed, and distributed entirely by Japanese.

It was at Osaka that I made my own *début* as a dancer, an unpaid performance which occurred under somewhat unusual circumstances, and in a somewhat unusual setting.

Having only about five minutes to reach the theatre before the rise of the curtain, I dashed into a rickshaw. When I had taken my seat it was to discover that for the life of me I could not remember the seven-syllabled word which represented the name of the theatre where we were performing. The rickshaw coolie glanced at me in enquiry, and I gazed back at him in despair. In the meanwhile the moments were passing. Something had to be done about it, and done quickly. Suddenly I had a brain-wave.

With more agility than I was accustomed to display I jumped from the rickshaw, and confronted the dumbfounded and apprehensive coolie with a really smart pirouette on one toe, followed by gestures indicative of the manipulation of flowing skirts. I am sure that had Pavlova been present she would have been struck dumb with jealousy.

OUR THEATRE IN OSAKA DISPLAYING PAVLOVA'S PLAYBILLS

Moreover, it did the trick. After gazing at me as if divided in his mind whether to bolt before I became really violent, or give me in charge of the nearest policeman, comprehension suddenly dawned on my rickshaw coolie.

He nodded, his face beaming, and motioned me to return to my seat. Then without hesitation he took me straight to the stage door of the theatre !

Another small but somewhat embarrassing experience occurred a few minutes before the curtain went up for our first performance at Tokio. The stage hands were sweeping as I walked across the stage, and the dust getting into my throat, I sneezed violently—with the result that the palate containing my only two false teeth shot meteorically across the stage. When I went to retrieve it, it was only to discover that it was broken.

Now, the gaps occasioned by that catastrophe happened to occur where they would be most noticeable ; where, also, they affected my speech to the point of incoherence. I could not possibly go into my seat unaccompanied by such important equipment. Fortunately, as safeguard against just such a mishap, I had long since provided myself with a duplicate plate. I glanced at my watch, and discovered that with ordinary luck I should have time to go back to the hotel and fetch my reserve stock before the time advertised for the rise of the curtain.

And the first people I met as I dashed across the vestibule of the Imperial Hotel were Sir Edgar

Iliffe and his daughter, with whom we had travelled on the same boat to Japan. Of course, he stopped me.

"My word, Stier," he said, "why aren't you at the theatre ? I thought the curtain rose at eight o'clock."

I must have looked as guilty as a schoolboy caught robbing an orchard. Usually (I hope) of truthful habit, now the truth was impossible. I whistled something through the gap, which even then I was on my way to fill, about having left an important orchestral score in my bedroom, and hurried discomfitedly away.

If it should reach the eye of Sir Edgar the above may serve both for explanation and apology.

We left Japan with genuine regret, and because hospitality had been so generous, laden with the presents it is the custom to place before each visitor to a private house. Some day I hope to renew my acquaintance with that sunny and smiling land, and my friendship with a sunny and smiling people.

China did not appeal to us in anything like the same way as Japan had done. It may have been that after the enthusiasm we had left behind the comparative indifference to our performance in Shanghai, Hong-Kong, and Singapore was somewhat disconcerting. Certainly the theatres were crowded each night, and by particularly appreciative audiences, but in each case these were almost exclusively British and American. In some way we did not seem to be able to establish any point of contact with the Chinese themselves.

At that time Shanghai was at the height of its prosperity, and of all the cities in the world we visited was by far the cheapest to live in. Particularly was that the case in the matter of transport. A rickshaw coolie, for instance, would take one almost any distance for a matter of ten cents. It was in connection with this means of transit that an incident occurred which, so far as Pavlova was concerned, contributed chiefly to her discomfort during our stay in China. It happened in Shanghai.

During the day we had paid a visit to the bazaar, which we found by far the most beautiful, besides the cheapest, of those we encountered in the East. There were so many things we wanted to buy that it was an impossibility to carry them back to our hotel. We made a few purchases, and promised to return for more on the following day.

Driving home from the theatre in a rickshaw that same night the coolie demanded a fee slightly in excess of the recognised rate. He became so insistent at last that he attracted the attention of a Sikh policeman, who, without listening to a word of his explanation, hit the unfortunate coolie over the head with his baton, and left him lying insensible in the road.

That incident alone was sufficient to give Pavlova a lasting dislike to Shanghai, and, to only a little lesser extent, to China in general. From that day, except for the theatre, she refused resolutely to leave her hotel. Also, I'm afraid the journalists who called to interview her did not obtain very much material for their trouble; at all events so far as her Art or plans for the future were concerned. Her whole mind and heart were obsessed with the piece of gratuitous cruelty she had witnessed, and she had no least hesitation in giving her opinion of the incident for publication.

The only drop of sweetness in the cup of her bitterness, so far as Shanghai was concerned, was that the hotel at which we stayed was run by a Russian refugee, who, escaping from his native country only after incredible hardship, had established himself in China, and with whom Pavlova lost no time in establishing a bond of sympathy.

Nor was our departure from the city without incident. Volinine, at that time Pavlova's dancing partner, caught the boat only by a hair's breadth. During our sojourn he had struck up a friendship with the Russian Consul there, from whom he received considerable hospitality, and who, on our very last morning, insisted upon giving him lunch.

Before setting off to fulfil the engagement Volinine was warned very solemnly of the exact moment of sailing, and, with a knowledge of his somewhat casual disposition and the Consul's reputation for hospitality, urged on no account to be late for the boat.

The time came for the rest of the company to embark. There was no Volinine, and as the time drew near to cast off, Pavlova's anxiety increased. The Consul's house overlooked the quay, and from the moment she stepped on board her eyes watched that residence unceasingly.

The whistle blew, the gangway was taken in, our propeller churned the water. Then, down the quay-side we discerned a flying figure who in each hand bore a large and closely packed suitcase. By the time he reached the point of embarkation we were at least eight feet from the quay. Without a moment's hesitation, still with a bag in each hand, Volinine hurled himself through the air, and by the grace of God and his own muscular development landed safely on deck. Having recovered his balance, quite unperturbed, he looked smilingly into the blanched face of Pavlova.

" You know I never could withstand a champagne lunch," he said genially.

Of Hong-Kong, which was our next port of call, I remember little except that I bought four jade buttons, and that Pavlova did not buy a shawl.

It was really a most exquisite piece of work, that shawl, and Pavlova coveted it. The price, however, was two hundred dollars, and for some reason I was never able to discover, it occurred to her that this was more than she could reasonably afford. Very reluctantly she turned away from the shop.

During the remainder of that day, however, she was unusually quiet—thinking it over. Eventually, as I had foreseen would be the case, she decided that extravagance was the better part of valour, and went post-haste back to the shop.

The shawl was gone.

That same night there was a dance given at the hotel, with the girls of our company as guests of honour. After the festivities had been in progress for some little time, Pavlova looked in. The first thing she saw was " her " shawl—on the shoulders of Muriel Stewart, a very talented and popular member of our company.

When we reached Singapore I left the four jade buttons I had bought in Hong-Kong to be made into cuff links. When I called for them I was told that the work would cost me five pounds.

I remonstrated. The charge was grossly excessive, and I had no hesitation in saying so. The proprietor of the shop, a large and stern-looking gentleman with a strong Caledonian accent, shrugged his shoulders. Five pounds was his price, he said, and if I wanted to take the links away, that is what I would have to pay. Eventually, under protest, I handed over the money, took my cuff links, and my departure.

After the first interval two or three evenings later a card was handed in at my dressing-room. As the name was quite unknown to me I sent a message to the effect that at the moment I was too occupied to interview strangers. When, however, at the next intermission the card was returned to me with the plea that I should be granting a great favour by sparing my caller a few moments on a matter of real importance, my curiosity was aroused to the extent of instructing the attendant to show the gentleman up.

When my visitor appeared he proved to be none other than the proprietor of the jeweller's shop whom I considered had treated me so shabbily in the matter of the links, though by this time his manner had undergone considerable change. The truculence which had distinguished his demeanour at our last interview was submerged, now, to diffidence and apology.

" When I charged you five pounds for those links," he said, " I had no idea whom I was dealing with. It was only in the theatre to-night that I recognised you. Had I done so at first I should never have dreamed of making such a charge." He paused, and then added ingenuously : " As a matter of fact, the day you left the work to be done a boat had come in with four hundred American tourists, and I mistook you for one of them ! "

My own manner, which at the onset had not been too genial, had thawed by this time ; it was impossible to remain hostile in face of such an attitude. I murmured something conventional.

" I cannot insult you by offering to return the money," he went on, " but I shall take it as a personal favour if you will call in at the shop and choose any article from my stock as proof of your forgiveness."

Of course I had no intention of doing anything of the kind, but happening to be passing the establishment a day or two later, the proprietor was standing at the door. Before I could protest he had ushered me inside We compromised at

L

last on a fountain pen, which I may say is in use to this day.

Smoking a friendly cigarette after this satisfactory termination of an originally unpleasant incident I happened casually to enquire where he had been born, though in view of his pronounced Caledonian accent the enquiry might well have been regarded as superfluous. To my amazement, however, he said : " Vienna."

When I told him that was the city from which originally I myself had embarked on my bid for fortune, it was clear from his manner that he would have been glad to have converted my jade buttons for nothing, and presented me with a small bonus into the bargain.

The man's history was interesting. Leaving Vienna at an early age for Glasgow, he had made the not uncommon discovery that it is easier for a foreigner to earn sufficient money to reach Scotland than, once there, it is to prise sufficient emolument from the inhabitants to enable him to leave.

However, he had accomplished even this super-human feat at last, and emigrating to Singapore, had obtained a minor position in a jeweller's shop. Once installed, and, one may presume, by the employment of those qualities which had enabled him to get away from Glasgow still in possession of sufficient money to pay his fare to China, and which, incidentally, had led him to charge five pounds for a job that would have been well paid for with half that amount, he had laid siege to the heart of his master's daughter, married her, and, his employer duly gathered to his father's, become proprietor of the business.

I have always thought since that an appropriate name for that man would have been Herr Richard McWhittington!

We were unfortunate in arriving at Singapore simultaneously with the production of a play by the local Amateur Dramatic Society, who had engaged the only theatre for that purpose. It was represented to the Society that it would be a graceful act on their part to postpone the performances in our favour, a suggestion to which they returned a polite but unequivocal refusal. This was the more annoying as, the theatre being closed practically the whole year round, they would have had no difficulty in arranging for whatever other dates would have met their convenience. It was on account of this prior claim that we were reduced to playing in a German club, and on a stage about the size of a lodging-house bedroom that was entirely devoid either of curtain or lighting.

In spite of these limitations we were advised that the Governor, His Excellency Sir Lawrence Guillemard, with whom we had travelled on the *Empress of Canada*, was desirous of attending a gala performance.

We got into communication with the manager of the club regarding the arrangements, and received a definite assurance that by seven o'clock on the day of the performance the stage would be in entire readiness: lighting, curtain, and all complete.

That man was a natural optimist, because when at the hour mentioned we arrived at the Club, it was to discover that nothing whatever had been done—there was neither curtain nor lights. Nothing remained, then, but to telephone our apologies to the Governor, and request that he would postpone his arrival until adequate preparation had been made for his reception. It was typical of the kindness with which everywhere we were received by British officials that although it was not until ten-fifteen that all was in readiness, his courtesy and good temper remained entirely unaffected by the delay. Pavlova, indeed, received a pressing invitation to stay at Government House, hospitality which, however reluctantly, she was obliged to refuse in order to leave herself free to attend rehearsals at any time she wished. So, as the next best thing, Sir Lawrence gave a dinner in her honour, to which I also was invited.

As is not uncommon in the East, there was a minority of ladies present. My own next-door neighbour was the Governor's physician. Conversation with this gentleman was of particular interest on account of his enthusiasm for chamber music, of which he had an intimate knowledge. When I complimented him upon this, and spoke of my own good fortune in having a dinner partner with whom I had so much in common, he told me with a twinkle in his eye that our juxtaposition was by no means accidental; that knowing his

PAVLOVA IN SINGAPORE

Facing page 164

propensity, the Governor-General himself had arranged that I should be the " lady " his physician took in to dinner.

From Shanghai we went on to Manila in the *Tayo Maru*.

Pavlova's aim in the East was to convert her audiences to an appreciation of the inherent significance and artistic possibilities of the art of the dance. In Japan she achieved this aim in a manner which far exceeded her dreams. In Manila she failed.

For though the Philippinos are great lovers of opera and song, outside their national dances this sister art meant nothing to them, and their reception of us was correspondingly cold. In addition our work was hampered by the perfectly appalling heat, which rendered it possible to rehearse only from eight until ten in the morning.

Nor was our life rendered more easy by the scorpions, mosquitoes, and enormous spiders which everywhere infest Manila, a scourge in no way mitigated by our hotel having only holes in the walls instead of windows, and that the doors were built on the Venetian blind system, a principle which gave free access to any crawling thing in search of accommodation or a free meal.

Socially, at least, the one bright spot was the Army and Navy Club, over which the Commandant of the troops, Colonel Bishop, so hospitably presided.

But the prince of all hosts was the Falstaffian " Mayor " Brown, so nicknamed on account of his universal popularity. " Mayor " Brown, who must

have weighed at least twenty stone, had made a
very large fortune by supplying coal to the American
warships which came into the harbour, and this
fortune he spent with regal lavishness. There was
about him a large-heartedness which I defy anyone
to have resisted ; he was loved because of his own
love for human nature in general. To be in trouble
or unhappy was the greatest claim which could be
made either upon his time or his finances. There
was not a young officer of the garrison or of the
warships in the harbour who in time of stress did
not turn as naturally to " Mayor " Brown as the
needle of the compass turns to the Magnetic North.
He was, in fact, the most understanding and
sympathetic liaison officer between the junior ranks
and high authority it is possible to imagine—a
buffer against which, on account of his personal
influence, the waves of retribution for small pecca-
dilloes among the younger warriors beat in vain.

As may be expected his hospitality was practically
universal. He kept open house for everybody who
was anybody, either resident or visitor, in the whole
of Manila.

Before we left he arranged a supper which
apparently he had determined should be a farewell
entirely adequate to the occasion. Pavlova was
to be the guest of honour, with the principal senior
officers from the fleet and garrison to pay her
tribute. And on the night of the party " Mayor "
Brown was seriously ill.

Quite characteristically, however, he had left
instructions that on no account were the arrange-

ments to be disturbed by his absence. He had appointed Colonel Bishop as deputy, insisting that in every way he was to act as host ; that the whole proceedings were to take place precisely as originally had been arranged. As if, in view of his absence, and its cause, such a spirit was possible !

It has to be admitted, however, that so far as a substitute was possible for a host of such out-standing personality and charm, Colonel Bishop stepped gallantly into the breach. After supper he took us a tour of the very beautiful bungalow, a house redolent of the taste and hospitable instincts of its owner. In one of the rooms was a glass case containing a vast array of single specimens of ladies' footwear. Enquiry elicited that a peculiarity of our host was to insist that any lady guest who particularly appealed to him should leave behind one of her slippers as a memento of the occasion !

It was a coincidence that, after an interview with the Press in which in no uncertain terms she had given her opinion of American ballroom dancing, it was in Manila that Pavlova jazzed for the first time.

It was that charming girl and most accomplished dancer, Muriel Stewart, who was responsible. She herself was very keen on ballroom dancing, and as this was the principal diversion of Manila, had ample opportunity for enjoying it. For a long time she had set herself to convert me to her own taste ; and so insistently at last that eventually she overcame my prejudice to the extent of inducing me to practice with her each morning.

And one night in the private supper room of our

hotel, Pavlova, too, fell. At first she would dance with no one but myself, and rather diffidently at that. Afterwards, however, when she became more used to it, she would take other partners. Nevertheless I am sure that it never really appealed to her.

A large proportion of her time was occupied in Manila by a tour of the various schools and public institutions with a view to discovering exactly what influence, benevolent or otherwise, the Americans had exercised over their protectorate. The conclusions to which she came after an intensive investigation was that, particularly under the Governor-General-ship of General Good, the United States had brought nothing but good to the Philippines.

If I were asked to say which, of all the incidents of our sixteen years' association, was the one most nearly to sound the keynote of Pavlova's character, I should unhesitatingly point to one which occurred during our sojourn in Manila. One day I was walking with Pavlova and Pianowski, our assistant Ballet Master, when an argument broke out between them on the subject of Poland, which happened to be the latter's native country.

Entirely ignorant as I am of Russian, in which language the conversation was conducted, it was yet not difficult to perceive that upon this subject at least the two did not see eye to eye. From animation the talk became excited, and from excitement ascended cumulatively in scale until, knowing both protagonists as well as I did, I realised that breaking point was not far distant.

Nor was it. Suddenly Pavlova burst into a passion of tears and, scarlet with indignation, turned on her heel and walked swiftly in an entirely opposite direction from the one we were making for, leaving Pianowski dancing with rage on the pavement. So far as he was concerned it was evident that something would have to give somewhere. Outlet was discovered at last. With a gesture of ungovernable temper he seized the gold-headed Malacca cane which was his inseparable companion, broke it savagely across his knee, and hurled each end far down the sunlit street. Then with a snort of rage he strode away, leaving me standing speechlessly in the middle of the pavement. And that, for the moment, was that—except for my inward thanksgiving for not having been asked to take sides.

Of course, the storm died as quickly as it had arisen, and in a few days Pavlova and her assistant Ballet Master were as friendly as always they had been. With the former, however, one cloud remained. The fact that it was through her that Pianowski had destroyed his walking-stick worried her more than a little.

" Please, Maestro," she said to me, " find me another one for him, exactly the same as the one he—lost. An absolute replica, please, so that he will not know the difference."

So it was that for the next few months, in every fresh town we visited, I made a point of looking through all the shops that sold walking-sticks to see if I could not discover one which would entirely satisfy her purpose. And then, nine months later, in Nice, I discovered a stick exposed for sale that was an exact replica of the broken malacca. I hurried back to the hotel, and found Pavlova and M. Dandré at lunch.

" I have a pleasant surprise for you," I announced to the former.

Pavlova looked up from her soup.

" What is it, Maestro ? " she enquired.

" I have found the stick of Pianowski," I said.

Instantly she was bubbling with animation.

" Quick, let us go at once," she exclaimed, jumping from her chair, " before anyone else has time to buy it ! "

M. Dandré, in that placid way of his, proceeded to argue the probability of the stick having been on sale for some little time, and the unlikelihood of its purchase during the half-hour or so it would take to finish lunch. Delay, however, would not do for Pavlova. The possibility of someone else buying the stick existed, and she was not out to take chances. Nothing, then, would satisfy her but that she and I should take a taxi there and then to the shop.

She presented it to Pianowski as soon as he came in. Just at first he regarded it as a miracle, believing that his own old favourite had been restored to him. And it was difficult to say which of the two obtained more pleasure from the presentation, giver or receiver.

CHAPTER X

FROM Singapore we sailed on the *Edavanna* for Burma, where we were to open at Rangoon, a city of which the native inhabitants are the only people within my experience who have reduced the beautiful philosophy of liberty and fraternity to a working doctrine, and that without making a fuss about it.

We were, too, extremely fortunate in our hotel, the Strand, the only one in Rangoon for the exclusive use of Europeans, and which was run on the European principle.

The proprietor, an Armenian, was a quite surprising personality, and the very last word in hosts. In that part of the world entertainments commence very much later than is usual elsewhere, so that it was not uncommon for us to arrive back at the hotel at one or two o'clock in the morning.

But whatever the time, never once did we find him unprepared, or anything but smiling, efficient, and extraordinarily attentive. We discovered later that during our stay he was in the habit of going to bed very early, with instructions that he should be awakened shortly before the time we would be likely to return. Then he would get up, dress, and personally supervise our supper and see that we had everything which by any possibility we could need. Every night of our stay there were fresh flowers in our rooms, for which no charge was made on the bill. Also, and more surprising still, he refused resolutely to accept a penny for any wine drunk by any one of our party during the stay.

A curious coincidence which happened in Rangoon was that next to the posters announcing Pavlova's visit were pasted pictures of Sybil Thorndike, with whose husband, Lewis Casson, I had worked in the old days at the Court Theatre, with whom then I had forged a tie of close and understanding friendship, and whose musical director I am even at this time of writing. Certainly it was like a message from home to see, in far Rangoon, a reproduction of the features I knew so well in the flesh.

The morning following our opening night in Burma, Pavlova received a message of welcome from Sir Harcourt Butler, the Governor. Later, he very hospitably sent his Secretary and two of his carriages to enable us to be present at a religious festival which was then in progress, and which, on several stages simultaneously, consisted chiefly of dancing, which we watched from the comfort of the Royal box so kindly placed at our disposal. Truly it was a wonderful sight. The dancers, clad in the most beautiful and elaborate of native costumes, appeared to be absolutely untirable, for they danced for hours on end without the least sign of fatigue.

The audience, of many thousands, were as

interesting as the performers, and, threading their way between the serried ranks, were vendors of refreshments and, particularly, cigars at least fifteen inches long, which were smoked impartially by men and women alike.

The only fly in the ointment of our content in Rangoon was the illness of two of our girls, though so far as one of them is concerned, I'm sorry to say it was her own fault. In common with the rest of the company she had been warned of the pressing danger of sunstroke. Nevertheless, just before we left the boat, she insisted upon sitting without a hat during the very hottest hours of the day, and with the inevitable result. After a stay in hospital at Rangoon we were forced to send her home, and I doubt very much if ever she overcame the effects of that exposure. The other girl was affected rather badly with local fever, and sent to the same hospital. She, however, was soon quite all right again.

If it came to an exact declaration of taste I am inclined to think that Pavlova would vote for our tour through India and Burma as the most fascinating in her experience. From the first the country seized her imagination after a fashion I have not observed in her before or since. It was as though she loved to steep herself in the traditions and mysticism of the people ; mentally and spiritually to bathe in the ever-changing colour and age-old customs.

Speaking for myself, and though to a large extent able to identify myself with this appreciation, I am not quite able to go all the way with her. To me, Japan is the Queen of the East. My reason for this preference, I think, is that I am more at one with the Japanese philosophy of life than with either the Indian or Burmese, tolerant and understanding as undoubtedly the latter may be. There is in Japan a calm happiness of outlook which is not to be found to the same extent in our Indian possessions, one I am inclined to ascribe to an objective happiness as opposed to a passive acceptance.

Another factor which goes to influence my preference is that there is nothing like the same poverty in Japan as is everywhere to be seen in India. And if, reversely, there is not the same incredible wealth in Japan as that with which the Maharajahs of British India are possessed, neither is there the frightful and unending stream of those professional beggars, disfigured and mutilated at birth to render their appeal to the charitable more poignant, as is to be found in almost every Indian city. The sight of human beings without ears, with hands slit to the wrist, and toes to the ankle, of abdomens enlarged beyond semblance to humanity, was to me sufficient to mar all those other and more gorgeous spectacles for which the Indian Empire is so renowned.

My first surprise was to discover that, though from different causes, our performance had as small support from the native population in India as had been the case in China. The reason for the aloofness of the Chinese was to be found in their

sense of superiority. The reason for the aloofness
of the Indian was poverty, for the proportion of the
population in any Indian city who have money
for anything beyond the bare necessities of existence
must be extremely small. I may be wrong in this
—indeed, I have little sympathy for the writer
who poses as an authority on a country after only
a brief visit—but such was my impression, and it
is one that is not coloured in any way by paucity
of box-office receipts, which as a matter of fact
were very much more than satisfactory.

But, speaking generally, it was not from Indians
that this support came, but from Europeans and
Americans. And particularly was this the case in
Calcutta, which is by far the most Westerly in
custom of any city at which, up to that time,
we had stayed on the Asiatic continent.

One night we visited an Indian theatre for the
purpose of seeing the dancing of the Nautch Girls.
Rarely have I seen Pavlova so impressed—far more
so than she had been by a performance of the Geisha
in Japan. Actually, the movements of the Nautch
dancers were not very dissimilar to our own. In
addition, their costumes were a very miracle of
loveliness, and the exquisitely shaped feet of the
performers, each bearing a single gold anklet, were
at one with the rest of the performance.

To round off this perfection, too, was the native
music, which was of a clear melody and rhythm
far more inspiring than any we had heard since
leaving the Western world behind.

To Pavlova there was only one way fitting to

mark her appreciation of all this beauty—to prepare an Indian ballet for inclusion in her own répertoire. After mature consideration she decided that this should be entitled " Ajanta's Frescoes " (The Great Renunciation), a title that was inspired by frescoes in the Ajanta Temple. Once having come to this decision she set to work with her usual thoroughness to prepare her plans.

Her first thought was for music fitting to the theme. This obstacle she overcame by sending me to the native theatre with instructions to jot down any air which occurred to me as likely to be suitable. Then, with the kindly and invaluable assistance of Mr. W. E. Gladstone Solomon, Director of the School of Art in Bombay, she set herself to purchase the necessary costumes, which after considerable trouble and expense she succeeded eventually in doing. An additional ballet, " A Hindu's Wedding," arranged at the same time, is now one of the most artistically successful in her repertoire.

It was in Calcutta that we went very close to missing the most important of all our Indian engagements, and it was due only to the kindly and diplomatic offices of Captain Thomas Robbins, a cheery and understanding soul who at one time had been attached to the British Embassy in Berlin, and with whom during our stay in the city we had become fast friends, that we were able to extricate ourselves from what looked like being a most unfortunate *impasse*.

Owing to the tremendous heat, our matinée

PAVLOVA IN CALCUTTA

Facing page 176

performances did not commence until five o'clock in the afternoon. The last of the series Pavlova devoted to raising funds for her Children's Home in Paris, of which I have written previously. After the final curtain, and in order to enhance the success of the performance, she elected to auction autographed photographs of herself from the stage. Thus it was between a quarter and half-past seven before we left the theatre.

To enable us to fulfil a command performance at Delhi before Lord Reading, the Viceroy, our train was due to leave at 8.5 p.m. In quite good time, Volinine, Pianowski, and myself piled into a taxi to take us to Howra station. By the time our train was due to leave we were hopelessly lost.

Instead of in the correct direction, for some reason or other the driver took us right out into the country. He found the right road at last, but only to arrive at the station half an hour after the train had left.

We interviewed the stationmaster, but it was easy to see that we meant nothing in his young life at all. The train was gone, and as far as he was concerned that, indubitably, was that. Our fervently pressed claim to a special he laughed at merrily as one of the happiest jokes of recent years. By a stroke of good fortune Tommy Robbins, who had paid his adieus to Pavlova and the rest of the company, had waited to commiserate with our discomfiture, and to render whatever help he might be able to influence on our behalf.

Whom it was he persuaded the originally sceptical

M

powers-that-be we were, I have never been able to discover. All that mattered was that he impressed them with a sufficient sense of our importance to induce them to give us accommodation on a goods express, which left for Delhi a little later that same evening. Also, we were given *carte blanche* to stop the train whenever and wherever we liked; to regard it, in short, as a Royal Special. If any possible doubt could still have remained as to our friend's forethought and kindly feeling, that would have been most summarily dispelled when, a few moments before we boarded the train, he reappeared, after a brief absence, laden with a cargo consisting of three bottles of champagne, four bottles of whisky, two cases of bottled beer, and an enormous basket of sandwiches as sustenance for our journey. And so it was that, thanks to this cheery friend, we reached our destination in time for the engagement.

Nevertheless I was somewhat surprised at the building in which the company were called upon to perform, for it was merely the stable of a cinema hall, refurbished in honour of the occasion. Furthermore, by the time we reached the building, the cordon of detectives which surrounded it was so closely drawn that only with the utmost difficulty were we able to reach what did duty as a stage door. As a matter of fact the innermost circle of police resolutely refused to allow us to pass until M. Dandré had been fetched from the building to vouch for us.

By then there was no time for a rehearsal. Not

for the first time I was forced to rely on the efforts
of those three staunch Russian musicians who, it
will be remembered, had joined the company in
Japan, and right nobly did those loyalists rise to
the occasion.

Actually the affair was a conspicuous success.
Lord and Lady Reading sat immediately behind
me, so that I was able to judge from their applause
and the remarks which passed from one to the
other how genuine was their appreciation.

The following day was a holiday. We spent it,
as I suppose most visitors would have spent it, in
a visit to Agra for the purpose of seeing the Taj
Mahal.

In all I saw it three times, the first two by day,
the last occasion by moonlight, at two o'clock in
the morning.

In these reminiscences I have tried, so far as
possible, to avoid superlatives. I find it difficult
to retain that reticence in connection with this
truly wonderful achievement in beauty. Nor shall
I readily forget the emotion on Pavlova's face as
for the last time she turned away from it.

Recently I have been reading Mr. Aldous
Huxley's *Jesting Pilate*, and according to that the
Taj Mahal is all wrong. " Those four thin tapering
towers standing at the four corners of the platform
on which the Taj is built," the author gravely
states, " are among the ugliest structures ever
erected by human hands."

Well, it takes all forms of opinion to make a
world, and so far as concerns the beautiful and the

impressive not all of us see eye to eye. Which, in view of the opinion of this distinguished authority upon the Taj Mahal, is perhaps not altogether to be regretted.

From Agra the company went on to Bombay, which we found even more aggressively European than Calcutta, and this despite the fact that the city contains no less than seventy-three thousand Parsees, who are the most intelligent and enlightened of all the Indian people. Many of them are prosperous business men, all of whom speak fluent English. In the houses of those who were so hospitable as to hold receptions in our honour we were entertained more lavishly than in any throughout our tour. A fitting culmination to a memorable journey round the world.

It was in Bombay that Pavlova and I had an experience which neither of us are likely to forget. Out driving one day a marriage in progress near by arrested our attention, and we stopped our carriage the better to see it. A man standing in the vicinity, who obviously had recognised my companion, approached.

" Madame Pavlova," he said courteously, " would it interest you to be a witness of this wedding ? "

She replied that most certainly it would. Accordingly we alighted, to find that two brothers were being married to two sisters, and that there were present more priests than guests at the ceremony.

These priests looked singularly dignified and majestic, with their white beards and flowing white robes. So far as we could gather, one of the most important features of the service was the world-wide practice of showering the happy couples with rice, a ceremony which lasted for at least twenty minutes. Then were produced two basins filled with milk, in which the brides laved their feet. After which, at what obviously was the culminating moment, the little fingers of brides and bridegrooms were tied together with string. And that, as far as we could ascertain, was the completion of the ritual.

While in Bombay we were entertained by the Governor, Sir George Lloyd, now Lord Lloyd and High Commissioner in Egypt. He sent for Pavlova to take a seat in the Royal box, with himself and Lady Lloyd, at the race meeting.

I remember an incident that happened when, immersed in wonder at the kaleidoscopic medley of every imaginable colour which renders an Eastern race-course one of the most gorgeous and picturesque scenes in the world, Pavlova and I were strolling together in the paddock.

Suddenly Pavlova uttered a little cry of distress, and without a word rushed from my side to that of a jockey, who, having dismounted, and evidently disappointed at the animal's performance in the race, was cruelly belabouring it before leading it into the paddock. Forthwith she proceeded to preach him an indignant sermon in voluble French, of which, though obviously he was ignorant of the language, the purport was unmistakable. When, eventually, he was released from the lash of her tongue, he could not have been more solicitous towards his mount had he been the President of the R.S.P.C.A. himself.

Another sight, which to the end of my life will remain indelibly on my memory, was that of the vultures engaged in devouring the human bodies on the Tower of Silence in Bombay, with others of these loathsome birds, hundreds of them, perched on the surrounding trees. Of all chilling and revolting sights that is by far the most repellent I ever witnessed. I had an intense dislike for these scavengers before I saw this unutterably revolting spectacle; since then I have hated them more than I have words adequate to express.

The last native ceremony we witnessed was that of the wedding of a Hindu boy of eleven to a tiny girl of nine, and which, as it took place in an open courtyard in full view of the street, Pavlova stopped the carriage to watch. After a few moments she asked to be permitted to present the juvenile benedicts with a wedding gift, a request which was received with undisguised enthusiasm by the newly united couple. Ten rupees was the amount disbursed, which from the delight with which it was received, might have been a hundred times that amount. It was this ceremony which ultimately Pavlova turned to such good account in her Indian Ballet at Covent Garden.

CHAPTER XI

AFTER India, Egypt was our next *pied-à-terre*. We were three weeks in Cairo, and for that time basked in comparative tranquillity under the cloudless skies of a lovely climate.

The theatre we played in was the Kursaal, the directorate of which was Italian, with a mixed Italian-Greek orchestra. The audience was principally native, the women sitting in boxes quite apart from the men. They were dressed almost entirely in black, and apart from the eyes their faces were veiled. One pair of these eyes, at least, I found somewhat disconcerting.

In one of the lower boxes close to my seat was a woman whose eyes were so beautiful and so penetrating that literally they had almost an hypnotic effect upon me. I cannot account for it in the least; all I know is that the warning light to commence the overture flashed no less than four separate and distinct times before I quite realised where I was. Even then it was only to discover that I had completely forgotten the opening bars of the ballet I was supposed to be conducting.

A further factor at the Kursaal which failed to add to our comfort was that we played there during one of the periodical political disturbances which about that time were so prevalent in Cairo. It seemed to us that when a malcontent had determined to throw a bomb at a British soldier it was inevitable that he should choose as the scene of his bid for national freedom the immediate neighbourhood of the Kursaal, and invariably at a time when our performance was in full swing. Hardly was it surprising, then, to find our audiences becoming progressively less numerous, particularly as, irrespective of the Kursaal being the storm-centre of the disturbances, a large proportion of the population were afraid to venture into the streets at all.

The Pyramids seized upon Pavlova's imagination more strongly than any other single circumstance of our tour. Their effect upon her was such that above all things she needed to be alone. For this purpose, and so that she might see the sunrise, which at that time of the year occurs about 4 a.m., she determined to spend a night, entirely by herself, at the Mena Hotel, which stands on the very fringe of the desert.

Although it seemed unwise for a woman of her fame to be quite alone in so strange a place, her insistence upon doing so was such that we were obliged to give way. Before she set off she left a message to the effect that at four o'clock on the following afternoon she would be with us again. During that twenty-four hours those of the company who knew of her intention were somewhat on tenterhooks. And though, true to her word, she reappeared exactly at the time appointed, beyond stating that her experience had been quite unforgettable, she was wholly reticent as to her thoughts and feelings during the experience. I would have given much to have seen Pavlova's eyes as in that first flush of desert dawn she exchanged smiles with the spirit of eternal woman which is the Sphinx.

The next house at which we played was the modern and well-equipped Mohammed Ali Theatre in Alexandria. The orchestra there was excellent, with a Viennese leader and Italian personnel.

It was in Alexandria where an incident took place which, however trivial in itself, is yet interesting as being eloquent of Pavlova's attitude towards the moral code. Though I do not know a more genuine and whole-souled Bohemian than she, and in the best sense of a much abused term, reversely I know of no woman with a greater reverence for physical purity, or a more deeply seated disgust for casual or commercialised vice.

At a costume ball we attended Pavlova was persuaded, very much against her will, to offer a signed photograph of herself as the first prize for the most beautiful costume. It was unfortunate for her prejudices that this should have been won by a French lady more celebrated for her physical attractions than for the rigid orthodoxy of her daily life. I saw the warning flush mount to Pavlova's cheek and the set of her lips as the name of the prize-winner was announced.

When the successful lady came up to receive her trophy I was not surprised to hear Pavlova murmur an excuse to the effect that, the request to award the prize having been sprung upon her only after her arrival at the hall, naturally she had no photograph available until she could return to her hotel to procure one.

During the next few days the importunities of the French lady that she should receive her prize were only a little less insistent than Pavlova's evasions from handing it over. In the meanwhile the time was drawing near for the company to leave Alexandria.

At last the day came when we were actually on the boat. Even then, on the vessel itself, the French lady followed with a demand for the photograph. And once again, and finally, Pavlova proved too much for her.

"I can hardly sign a photograph here on the deck," she said. "Permit me to retire to my cabin where I can do so with more convenience."

But once in the seclusion of her own suite, there Pavlova remained until the vessel actually had left the quay.

"The thought of my photograph in the boudoir of that woman," she said to me in explanation, "was utterly intolerable."

Not infrequently I am asked if during our wanderings we ever had had a complete failure. My invariable reply is an emphatic affirmative. One failure we had, and one only. It was in the small town of Cien Fuegos in Cuba.

It was following a successful season in Havana that, having a few days to spare, it was suggested that it might be profitable to give performances in one or two of the neighbouring towns, and to this Pavlova gave assent.

We went first to Matanzas, some two hours' journey from Havana, where we had an enthusiastic reception from a very crowded house. Thus encouraged, we determined to try our luck at Cien Fuegos, four hours from Havana. We arrived to find the station entirely deserted. There were no taxis, nor, indeed, any form of vehicle to take us through the deserted unpaved streets, which were knee-deep in mud. Through this morass, carrying our hand baggage, we squelched our way to the hall where we were booked to appear.

There we discovered a dejected-looking custodian in charge of the box office. Pavlova approached him, and when at last she had penetrated his coma sufficiently to enable him to realise who she was, " How many tickets have been sold ? " she enquired.

" *One !* " he replied.

Pavlova gave a smile of pure joy. She handed the man a note.

" Return the gentleman his money with my sincere compliments and thanks," she said. Then she turned to us. " We will now return to Havana, and pass a really pleasant evening," she announced.

And with a whoop of joy we turned back to the station to await the next train.

I know no more attractive city than Havana. To me it combines the amenities of Paris, Vienna, and Budapest, with a fascination entirely its own. Essentially it is a city of pleasure, which lays itself out to cater for those to whom bed is only a necessary superfluity.

Some six years previous to my last visit, I had met in Spain a German-American by the name of May, and to whom I had shown some small hospitality. When I parted from him he had been insistent that if ever I happened to be in Havana— from where he was visiting Spain on business—I should give him the opportunity of making some slight return for what he was pleased to describe as my kindness.

On the occasion I refer to I was on my way to join Pavlova in New York. Our call at the Cuban capital was an enforced one of four days, while the ship discharged and loaded cargo, a delay which at first seemed likely to be more than usually irksome.

Then it was I recollected the friend I had made in Spain, and his pressing invitation for me to visit him. I did not know, after such a lapse of time, even, if he was still in Havana. However, it was worth trying, and I took a taxi to the street he had indicated as the one in which his office was situated. And there, sure enough, was his sign.

I paid off the taxi and mounted the stairs. My prospective host recognised me at once. Without more ado he turned to his two brothers, who since our last meeting had joined him in business, and to the lady typists busy over their machines.

"Now that Mr. Stier is here," he announced, " it gives us an excuse for closing the office for the

THE FIFTEEN-YEAR-OLD CARICATURIST OF HAVANA GETS TO WORK

Facing page 188

four days of his visit to enable us to show him the sights of Havana."

And that, actually, is what he did. My memory of the succeeding ninety-six hours is somewhat uncertain. I do not think there was a café or a dance hall we did not visit. In those four days I obtained precisely five hours' sleep.

The Ritz-Biltmore Hotel in Havana is one of the best at which we stayed throughout the world. After all, Havana is only a couple of days from New York, and in the Cuban capital there is no prohibition. Hence the unceasing procession of Americans with dollars to burn and thirsts to quench—and the luxurious Ritz-Biltmore Hotel.

On an earlier visit to Havana in 1917, Pavlova found herself booked to appear in the middle of a strike of policemen, a demonstration which was conducted with a ferocity only possible in a Latin country, and in which revolvers and other small-arms were the predominant argument. It takes a brave woman to fulfil an engagement each night through even desultory bullets, and many times the firing was very far, indeed, from casual. Even then it was not from any desire of her own that the evening performances at the famous Pyrat Theatre were cancelled, but from economic necessity. After all, the majority of people will pause before running the gauntlet of revolver shots, even to see the greatest dancer in the world. The few matinées which with characteristic courage and determination she decided to give were practically without audience.

It was a relief, then, to escape to Don Jose, the capital of Costa Rica, there to act in a theatre which, because the wealthy Costa Rican who built it was in love with a Frenchwoman, is an exact replica of the Paris Opera House.

At Quayaquil, Ecuador, Pavlova found herself for the first time performing in a town which, owing to the prevalence of bubonic plague, is in a state of perpetual quarantine. I am glad to be able to place on record, however, that our company escaped bubonic and every other plague except the plague of mosquitoes.

Lima, the capital of Peru, a town of only a hundred and twenty thousand inhabitants, saw one of our greatest successes. For four whole weeks the theatre was filled to capacity at each performance. It was here, also, that local enthusiasm took the form of a public subscription for the presentation to Pavlova of a plaque inscribed in gold.

Leaving Lima, the company played for three weeks in Valparaiso, and following a similar period in Santiago, crossed the Andes to spend a month in Buenos Ayres. After Buenos Ayres, Caracas was the next stopping-place, where it will be remembered President Gomez presented Pavlova with the velvet-lined jewel case upon the top of which her name was worked in twenty-five dollar pieces. It was here, however, as a rather amusing contrast to that gesture, that there was not a bank in the town at which M. Dandré's attempt to change an American thousand-dollar bill was met with anything but a blank refusal. Eventually he was obliged to part with it at very considerable loss through one of the local pawnshops.

From Caracas, on to Venezuela, where the company met with considerable success, and from thence to Porto Rico, where Pavlova enjoyed a two months' rest before opening at Para, a town that is situated exactly on the equator.

Here I am inclined to think that there is more variety of insect life, and of greater individual proportions, than in any place in the world. Even the stage itself was invaded each night by vedettes from the standing army of giant spiders and beetles, and to an extent which would have frightened a lesser woman than Pavlova.

" The very butterflies are as big as seagulls," she remarked on one occasion.

It was here, and during her visit, that a memorial in her honour was unveiled in the local theatre. To the general surprise she refused resolutely to go and see it.

" It may be foolish," she explained, " but I am superstitious of memorials to the living."

I did not think it necessary to remind her that it is almost impossible to pass from Victoria Station to Victoria Street without a sight of the replica of herself which, poised on tip-toe, stands on the summit of the Victoria Palace Music Hall.

The end of the War saw us at Panama on our way back to the United States.

This was a journey I do not think anyone in the company will readily forget. At Panama the

Americans were stopping all boats, and from thence employing them to carry food to Europe. So here the company were obliged to kick their heels for twenty-one solid days.

At the end of that time word was obtained of a tiny French cargo boat loaded with saltpetre for Cuba. There was, so the word went, room on the craft for eight passengers. Actually she carried sixty-four, with the Pavlova Company included among those present. And as all accommodation was swallowed up many times over before we had even heard of the boat, it was necessary for M. Dandré to purchase washing basins, blankets, and other indispensable accessories for the whole company, the majority of whom, and all the men, being required to sleep on deck.

However, Santiago was reached at last—and there a general strike was in progress. All traffic was at a standstill, and everything else in a state of chaos.

Here the company waited for a week, at the end of which the Governor ordered a special train for our accommodation, with soldiers in armoured cars to guard the luggage.

For three days and nights this journey was beset at every stage by armed strikers. Half the journey accomplished, we arrived at a point where terrorism prevailed, and deciding to call it a day, the driver deserted the train. The situation was relieved at last by a negro stage hand undertaking to carry on to Havana for a fee of ten dollars *per diem.*

And when at last Havana was reached it was to be pitchforked into the centre of another general strike.

By this time, plucky as they were, the nerves of the lady members of the company were on the point of giving out. Except for the stairs upon which, because it was that or nothing, they were obliged to sleep, there was no room in the hotels.

We were warned, even then, that it would be extremely dangerous to attempt to reach the United States through Mexico. However, strings were pulled, and at last promise of safe conduct was obtained from Carenza himself, and so it was decided to risk it. The company reached Vera Cruz to find the promise had been vindicated to the extent of a special train having been reserved for us, and that this was protected by a bodyguard of a hundred and fifty soldiers, who rode on the roofs of the cars all the way to Mexico City.

Nevertheless, and grateful as we were for the protection, our minds were not unduly uplifted by the sight of the corpses which hung from the telegraph poles practically throughout the route. Whether these unfortunates were strikers or anti-strikers we were never able to discover. Probably a few of each, I should imagine.

N

CHAPTER XII

IT is doubtful if any audience displays quite the same enthusiasm for Pavlova as obtains in Madrid. There is, too, a picturesqueness in this appreciation which appeals directly to Pavlova's sense of romance. For of all places it is here where they " say it with flowers " ; there were performances in the Spanish capital when the stage was literally covered with blossom.

The King of Spain was one of the most loyal supporters of Pavlova's art, and never once visited the theatre but to send her a bouquet.

A peculiarity of the Spanish theatre is that the performance does not commence until half-past ten, and that to allow society to follow the immemorable custom of exchanging visits from box to box, the *entr'acte* lasts for over half an hour. Thus, on our own visits there it was usually well into the early hours of the morning before we found our way back to the hotel.

Of the many interesting and amusing people we met in Madrid perhaps the most striking was Fernandez Arbos, a former professor at the Royal Academy of Music in London, and who not infrequently conducted the Sunday concerts at the Albert Hall. He is artist and linguist, musician and humorist.

One of his chief delights, and one which used to reduce Pavlova almost to tears of laughter, was to perform his parody of her Swan dance. A dying swan wrapped in a tablecloth, and with an enormous black beard, is hardly the height of realism ; nevertheless there was real genius and irresistible fun in the representation.

It was in his house where, also, we met most of the contemporary Spanish artists and writers, and hence both Pavlova and myself found the atmosphere unusually congenial. As did, incidentally, Señor Arbos's wife, a French lady who had not succeeded in reconciling herself to the seclusion in which Spanish ladies are expected to pass their lives.

Another interesting personality—and, his idiosyncrasies understood, only a little less entertaining —was a certain aristocrat whose house was filled with a most wonderful collection of sculptuary and paintings. Thus, when in a gesture in which was included the whole of the assembled masterpieces, he claimed them as his own work, I was conscious of a thrill of admiration.

" Me—I did them," he announced with rather more than a touch of pride.

With no reason to question the authenticity of his claim, my admiration led me a little later to refer to this genius when chatting with a group of his friends. They smiled benignly.

" Just his little way," one of them explained charitably, " due, no doubt, to his enthusiasm. A great patron of the arts, as, probably, you understood. He himself, however, is neither painter nor sculptor. Nevertheless it pleases him, this self-deception that he has painted or chiselled everything he buys." An expressive and entirely Spanish gesture followed, indicating tolerance. "Just his little weakness," my informant added, "and because it means so little, with no harm attached. As I have said, he is a great patron of the arts."

If one story current about this enthusiast is correct, however false may be his claim to personal fame, at least it leaves no room to doubt his love for art. For it is said that upon an occasion, not so many years ago, he pleaded with the Pope himself for the loan of a group of figures from the Vatican so that he might make a copy. When the work was completed, so it is claimed, it was this copy which was returned to his Holiness, and the original retained. Than which enthusiasm for art could go no further.

Belgium is another country where appreciation of Pavlova's art is paramount. I remember in 1919, following a brief season in Liège, that when we went to settle with the various newspapers in which the performances had been advertised, to our astonishment they refused to accept payment for a single insertion.

"Pavlova has done so much for the national appreciation of art," they explained, "that we simply cannot bring ourselves to accept money from her."

But perhaps this is only typical of a Press who, during that same visit, combined to buy up every

PAVLOVA AND THE AUTHOR ENJOYING THE SUN AFTER LUNCH AT MANILA

Facing page 196

available flower in the city for the audiences to throw on the stage as tribute.

Another recollection of Liège, though a little less pleasant, is of the theatre librarian, an appointment, it may be mentioned, which is the prerogative of the Town Council under whose jurisdiction rests the administration of the Municipal Opera House.

In every city I visit I make a point of enjoying a long conversation with the librarian of the theatre. A matter of necessity this, for upon this official devolves the duty of preparing the orchestral parts in their correct order, and subsequent distribution to the many departments of the orchestra.

But when in Liège I made my usual request for an interview with the librarian, to my astonishment I was presented to an old lady of seventy-five; unfortunately, also, one whose years were more venerable than her knowledge of her job was accurate. Which, considering the specialised nature of the work, is hardly a matter for surprise. Apart from an exact knowledge of music and composers the theatre librarian should be something of a linguist; it must be remembered that more often than not the titles of the scores are inscribed in a foreign language.

After five minutes' somewhat disjointed conversation with the lady, then, I suggested it would be more satisfactory to both of us if she took three days' holiday while I carried on with the good work, a suggestion to which she subscribed with alacrity and relief. To myself remained only to stay up the whole of one night for the purpose of reducing

the welter of music into something less approxi-
mating the last day of a jumble sale.

It was during our stay in Liège, and in connection
with this same librarian, that a most disconcerting
incident occurred, though fortunately it was one in
which the Pavlova Company was not immediately
concerned. It occurred to the Director of the
Opera House to stage a performance of " Manon,"
and that he himself should conduct ; further, that
the leading lady should sing an interpolated number.

It was not until the cantatrice had walked
majestically on to the stage and emitted the first
few bars of melody that it was discovered the dear
old lady librarian had inserted the additional
number in the music of half the members of the
orchestra, and completely omitted it from the
others, a lapse which, of course, was the forerunner of chaos, and with most lamentable results.
While the vocalist burst into a storm of tears and
dashed off the stage, the Director burst into a
flood of vituperation against the librarian, a tirade
of which we, in the stage box, were privileged to
hear every word.

Upon that occasion my sympathies were very
much with the singer. It was a fellow feeling ; I,
too, had experienced what it was to face an audience
under awkward conditions. And, curiously, the
episode I had in mind occurred in Belgium also—
in Brussels, as a matter of fact.

And of all good times and places it was at a
Gala Performance before the King and Queen.
The occasion was a matinée at The Royal Opera

House in aid of the Fund for Russian Refugees
from the Bolshevics, and for an official occasion
of such importance full evening dress was *de
rigueur*.

Immediately after lunch, then, I changed into
a dress suit and drove down to the Opera House
in a taxi. And as I was groping in my pockets for
the fare, another taxi drove up and knocked me
down. When I had gathered myself together,
though I was unhurt as to my person, my beautiful
white shirt front was bespattered with mud as to
at least a third of its surface. And this was five
minutes before the time fixed for the rise of the
curtain.

There was no help for it. Mud or no mud I had
to take my place in the orchestra, and although
by the aid of a penknife blade I accomplished
whatever refurbishing was possible, the result
remained still lamentable. Worst of all was that
upon the entrance of the King and Queen it was
essential for me to swing round in my place so as
to face that packed house as I conducted The
National Anthem—with a mosaic of road surface
on my otherwise immaculate bosom.

It was in 1912 that we had arranged to open at
The Opera House in Berlin. Just as I was on the
point of leaving London I received a telegram
from Herr Leonard, Pavlova's manager for
Germany, which ran :

" CANNOT GET GOOD HARPIST. BRING ONE
ALONG."

That was an instruction it was more easy to

give than to carry out. Considering that these instrumentalists are paid the highest possible salaries, and do very little work, their scarcity is remarkable. Nevertheless the fact remains that a good harpist is an extremely rare bird indeed.

In this instance I made enquiries from all the recognised sources in London, and these failing, from any other quarter which by any chance might prove profitable, and without a glimmer of success. And then, at the eleventh hour, I received information that residing in Bristol was an extremely gifted harpist, and whom it was possible might be procured.

So off I dashed to Bristol, where I discovered the lady to be the daughter of a locally famous physician. However, I put my pride in my pocket, and, figuratively, went down on my knees to her father to gain his consent to the girl accompanying us to Berlin. Eventually, with obvious reluctance, and after an examination of my own credentials which would have done credit to a professional analyst, he consented. In due course, then, " Padgy," as afterwards we came to call her, set off on her journey with the company.

At our opening performance Dr. Richard Strauss and Arthur Nikisch sat immediately behind me. After the curtain descended on the last act, Strauss asked me to present him to Pavlova. On our way behind the scenes he turned to me : .

" Who is your harpist ? " he demanded. " Certainly she is a most extraordinary artist."

" That extraordinary artist," I informed him,
" is an English amateur."

Strauss looked surprised, as well he might. He
was silent for a moment, then :

" English amateur or not," he said, " I'm very
anxious to obtain her for the Berlin Philharmonic."

I confess I was not very hopeful, but I did my
best by introducing Strauss to Padgy. If only
from an added experience as to the possibilities
of the human expression it was worth while to
have done so. I shall never forget the look on
Strauss's face as at long last he was brought to
realise that the unprecedented honour he was
conferring upon this unknown English harpist
cut no manner of ice with her at all.

Her attitude, had he been able to realise it, was
perfectly simple and straightforward. She had
come to Berlin to oblige me, and in Berlin she
would remain until the end of our season. That
finished, so far as concerned any idea of adopting
her art as a profession she, also, was finished. She
was very comfortably situated at home, where she
was very happy indeed, thank you very much.

And that was that.

Arrived at Düsseldorf following our Berlin season,
I was almost incredulous when I was informed that
there was no Symphony Orchestra available. There
was nothing for it, then, but to fall back upon the
local Postmen's and Railway Porters' Bands. And
as the men were working all day it was necessary
to conduct rehearsals at midnight.

Cassel, in Germany, was the only place where,

apart from Japan, the musicians stood to attention on my appearance, and so remained until it occurred to me to stand them at ease. This is accounted for by the fact that we had found it necessary to engage a military band. It is an illuminating side-light on pre-war German mentality that after rehearsal I should have been called aside by the bandmaster, who implored me not to address his men as " Gentlemen," or, in speaking to them, on any account to say " please."

" It would be the ruin of all discipline," he declared gravely.

It was during our German tour in 1914 that the audiences were so enthusiastic that in more than one town we were obliged to have police protection from their demonstrations.

On May 14th of that year we gave a command performance, consisting of " The Magic Flute " and Weber's " Invitation to the Dance," with *divertissements* which included the " Dying Swan " and the " Butterfly." The occasion was an historic one, being in honour of the birth of an heir to the Grand Ducal House of Brunswick.

It is well known that for many years there had been considerable tension between the Royal Hollenzollerns and the House of Brunswick, feeling which not altogether had died down with the alliance between the Duke and the only daughter of the Kaiser. Now, however, that the marriage had been blessed with an heir, it was regarded as politic to show the world that the hatchet was finally buried. Perhaps it was for that reason the audience present on the occasion consisted almost exclusively of reigning princes and their entourage.

Before the curtain rose for the first act the whole company was paraded before the Master of Ceremonies for the purpose of receiving instruction as to the rigid etiquette which would prevail for the occasion. This official was a most ornate person of considerable bulk, and covered with orders and sashes and every kind of decoration. As I was the only member of the company with a working knowledge of German it was to me that his remarks were chiefly addressed.

" First," he said, " you must understand that there will be no applause at any stage of the performance. Also—and this is of the greatest importance—it is vital that the overture shall commence at the exact moment the Emperor takes his seat ; neither a fraction of a second sooner nor an instant later "—a warning I was better able to appreciate after I had learnt that only a short time previously the conductor at the Royal Opera House in Berlin, Herr Emil Pauer, had been instructed to send in his resignation for no other reason than because, being engaged in wiping his glasses at the instant the Emperor took his seat, the opening bars of the overture were delayed by no less than twenty seconds.

As may be expected I took especial care there should be nothing of that kind occur at this command performance. Nevertheless it was more than a little disconcerting when the end of the first two ballets were followed only by an intense and formal silence.

And then, in the *divertissement*, when in the " Swan " Pavlova took her dying breath, the stillness was broken by the deep voice of the Emperor himself, exclaiming : " Wunderful ! Wunderful ! Bravo ! Bravo ! "

With such an example, how could the audience remain silent ? The brilliant assemblage broke into one of the most spontaneous and tumultuous ovations of which Pavlova was ever the recipient. And at the end of the performance she was called to the Royal box, and following a few moments' conversation I saw her, from my seat in the orchestra, bend down to kiss the hand of the Kaiserin.

Naturally we were all more than a little gratified at the success of our efforts, self-congratulation which, incidentally, did not appear to have communicated itself to the Master of Ceremonies, who seemed more than a little disgruntled that in the enthusiasm of the moment the tradition which forbade applause had been so spontaneously disregarded.

As soon as I was able I hurried round to Pavlova's dressing-room to congratulate her on her outstanding success. To my surprise I found her far from happy ; indeed, I never remember her being so depressed, or in quite the same fashion, as at that moment. It was a long time before I could induce her to tell me what either the Emperor or the Empress had said to her ; nor could I learn the reason for her depression. But that there was something she regarded very seriously weighing on her mind was only too obvious. Eventually I coaxed her into confiding the cause.

It appeared that when she had bent to kiss the hand of the Empress, she had left an impression from her rouged lips on the spotless white glove of the royal lady. And with the superstition of her race, Pavlova had read into that circumstance an omen of bloodshed.

Less than three months afterwards came the declaration of war, a tragedy which always Pavlova has declared to be the event foretold by that incident.

I am aware that this is not the first time the story has been told. To my personal knowledge these are the exact circumstances under which it took place.

From Germany the company went on to Vienna, an appearance to which I had looked forward for many years with the keenest anticipation. My parents were living in the Austrian capital, and it was my dear wish that they should be present at a performance of which I was musical director.

But it was not to be. For, the first night, when they would have been able to attend, try as I would I was not able to procure the necessary tickets, and thus was obliged to console myself with two boxes for the second performance. And on that very morning my father was taken suddenly ill. Before the time came when he should have been watching what I know would have been the greatest occasion of his life, he had passed away.

Actually I had to hurry from his death-bed to conduct a performance which, by one of those strokes of irony that occur in the lives of all of us, consisted of a humorous ballet !

CHAPTER XIII

I HAVE thought many times that quite an amusing book might be written on my ex-experiences with the various scratch orchestras it was necessary from time to time to collect to enable us to give our performances.

In Hastings, for example, I found I was required to assemble an orchestra from practically every amateur band in the town. This was accomplished at last, and with the exception of the lady drummer, with fairly satisfactory results. This lady, however, insisted upon taking her seat in the orchestra wearing a hat about three feet in diameter, and elbow-length white gloves; details of costume which would have been more excusable had she been capable of counting her bar's rest—which she wasn't. It was only after severe mental struggle that in the end I was able to brace myself to the point of asking her not to play at all. Whereupon she broke into a loud wailing noise and rushed from the theatre; this last, an act of grace for which I gave devout thanks.

It was in Harrogate where the muscular pains in my right arm which, through constant conducting, had for a long time been growing worse, reached a point of almost unbearable pain, a period when only Pavlova's personal devotion in massaging

207

the affected member enabled me to keep going at all. At the Yorkshire Spa, however, I took the bull by the horns and had electrical treatment for one single hour. Extraordinary to relate, since then I have had no single twinge of pain. Harrogate advertises itself pretty extensively as a health resort, and if my own experience is anything to go by, not without the fullest justification. Something in the air alone seemed to put new life in me.

Speaking generally, we found English audiences generous in overlooking any deficiency which quite obviously could not have been avoided. A good instance of this occurred at Scarborough, where the curtain rose just an hour and twenty minutes later than the advertised time.

We had been playing in Liverpool, and it occurred to Pavlova that it would be an agreeable change to travel from there to Scarborough by road. And for that day, at least, the very devil was in our car.

Time after time it broke down, and time after time Volinine, whose pride in his knowledge of engineering was not quite commensurate with his skill, tinkered about with it, but never to a point which rendered it a reliable vehicle of travel.

So it was that we reached Scarborough at nine-twenty for a performance which had been due to start at eight o'clock. In the intervening eighty minutes the orchestra, as it is the custom of orchestras, had stepped loyally into the breach by playing solos and duets and trios—anything

in fact which by any stretch of forbearance might
be calculated to keep the crowded audience in
good humour.

And most nobly the audience rose to the occasion, for when eventually, tired, dusty, hungry, and
unwashed, we presented ourselves, it was to gain
a reception as enthusiastic as if we had been
returned explorers from an Antarctic Expedition.

Another occasion when we were late, though
fortunately this time no performance was involved,
was when we started from Eastbourne at half-
past ten to keep a supper appointment with Lydia
Kyasht at the Savoy Hotel in London.

We had not been on the road very long before
the surrounding country became blotted out by
one of the densest fogs within my experience. It
became so bad at last I advised Pavlova that the
only thing to do was to make our way to the
nearest railway station to await the next train for
London.

But this Pavlova refused resolutely to do;
above all things she hates turning back from anything she has once undertaken. And thus it was
that, with our necessarily slow speed, and the fact
that it was necessary to swarm up practically every
sign-post to assure ourselves we were on the right
road, it was twenty minutes to seven in the morning
before, at long last, we reached the Savoy.

Here another calamity awaited us. In the whole
hotel there was only one bedroom that was not
already occupied. And though with characteristic
unselfishness Pavlova insisted that I should have

o

that room, I was only too glad to turn in on the sofa which, eventually, was found for me.

This alfresco couch is rather reminiscent of an experience to which the whole company was subjected at Bolton, in Lancashire, to where we travelled after an evening performance at Manchester.

We reached Bolton well after midnight, only to discover that a telegram had been sent by the manager there advising us to postpone travelling until the following morning, as no accommodation could be arranged for that night. Unfortunately, we had left Manchester before the delivery of the wire.

I can think of many more pleasant methods of spending the early hours of a winter morning than in wandering about an industrial town in Lancashire for the purpose of finding sleeping accommodation for over thirty people.

On that occasion, at least, Pavlova herself was fortunate, having stayed in Manchester with the intention of joining us by an early train the following morning. Actually, so far as her own peace of mind was concerned, it would not much have mattered had she been there to share in the experience. Where she has something definite to fight, she can meet any situation quite light-heartedly. It is the less tangible annoyances which prey most heavily upon her nerves.

I do not know if the same applies to-day, but at that time there was only one residential hotel in Bolton—at least, that we could hear of—and

that house was full. In the meantime, while our
deliberations had been proceeding, one or two of
the men had streaked off and found accommodation
on their own account.

But that did not in the least suit Edmund
Russon, Pavlova's English manager and my own
very good friend. With the unruffled efficiency
which characterises everything he does, and which
renders him such an invaluable representative of
the company's interests, he proceeded to take the
situation in hand.

Like a platoon of infantry in full equipment, and
carrying our suit-cases, we left the station in a
body. Commenced then a deliberate and intensive
comb-out for accommodation. Russon's first move,
however, was to call at the lodgings of the one or
two men who had found haven, and, leaving girls
in their places, to haul them incontinently forth.

Later, one by one, we found house room for the
other ladies, and not until the last of these was
installed would Edmund Russon permit a single
male member of the company to seek refuge.
When all the available rooms had been taken, but
with several men still without place to lay their
heads, we aroused the landlord of an ordinary
public-house, who fortunately proved to be of the
type of sportsman typical of the County Palatine.
He welcomed us whole-heartedly to the freedom
of his bar parlour where, seated on benches about
the sanded floor, the time was passed quite happily
until breakfast time in playing poker. The others
thus settled, I personally fared back to the Swan

Hotel. If in any nook or cranny of that caravan-serai remained one single bed, I meant having it.

The landlady, though charmingly good-tempered on being aroused from her own rest, was more than a little dubious.

" 'Appen we 'ave wun bed, sir, wi' no wun in it," she said doubtfully, in her native idiom, " buut t'Major's likely to be back any minute. 'E's nobbut gone to Man-chester."

" But he is not likely to be back as late as this," I argued.

" Ye nivver know—wi' t'Major," she said solemnly.

" In any case I'm prepared to take a chance," I announced.

The lady nodded ; still, however, dubiously.

" Awl reet," she said at last, " buut if t'Major coms back tha'll 'ave to clear out of his bed."

I am afraid the good faith was more inherent on her side of the bargain than upon my own, for I locked the door of the bedroom very firmly behind me before getting into bed. Thus, if " t'Major " had returned it is likely he would have been unlucky. However, as apparently he had found the attractions of " Man-chester " too much to his liking to return to Bolton, there was no harm done.

It was in Huddersfield Pavlova received a request from the Mayor that a deputation might wait upon her at the fall of the curtain. Pavlova raising no objection, the delegates in due course arrived. After a speech of warm welcome and congratulation the Mayor suddenly dived into his pocket and produced a large bottle of vodka.

" And we beg," he wound up, " that you will accept what, doubtless, to a lady of your nationality, is the most acceptable of all gifts we could have chosen."

It was in Newcastle-on-Tyne that on one Sunday night I remember casually dropping into a picture house with Pavlova. By some mischance the manager happened to be standing in the vestibule as we passed to our seats, and, it is to be presumed, recognised her. We had not been in our places two minutes before he walked on to the stage, stopped the performance, and announced impressively that they were honoured that evening by the presence of Madame Anna Pavlova, the greatest. . . . And so on.

Whereupon, to Pavlova's embarrassment and annoyance, the whole audience stood up in their seats and cheered to the echo.

Of our various seasons in London, two incidents stand out prominently in my mind. Each of them was more or less connected with a practical joke.

In a previous chapter I have mentioned the difficulty of obtaining competent harpists. There is, moreover, a similar dearth of really good trumpeters. This is because of the manner in which modern composers treat the trumpet, rendering it an extremely difficult instrument to play. Speaking generally, it is necessary to rehearse the performer intensively before anything like the correct standard of interpretation can be reached.

The trumpeter we had at Covent Garden, however, was little short of a genius; he seemed to be able to play the most difficult and complicated passages at sight. Briefly, the boy—a Londoner by birth—was the very best trumpeter of my experience.

His one drawback was—naturally perhaps, considering his youth—that knowledge of his own proficiency had tended rather to inflict him with that very distressing malady known as swelled head. Not aggressively, nor so as to be a nuisance to the rest of the orchestra; still, sufficiently to arouse the thought that it would be no very bad idea to bring him to a better sense of proportion.

One day he was given a passage to play, so difficult it was not thought possible for any trumpeter to correctly interpret without a considerable amount of practice. To the amazement of everybody, and incidentally to their covert admiration, the boy played it through perfectly the first time the part was placed before him.

"No difficulty at all about it," he explained airily to those unwise enough to pass comment on his brilliance. From then on he was perhaps a shade more aggressive in self-complacency than he had been before. Sufficiently so, at all events, to confirm the orchestra in the opinion that it was time he was brought to a better frame of mind.

Not far from the stage door of Covent Garden Theatre is a hostelry where members of the orchestra were accustomed to call in for occasional refreshment. Outside this hostelry, at a certain hour of

the day, an itinerant cornet player was in the habit
of entertaining the patrons within. To him one
of the orchestra took a copy of the especially difficult bars.

"How long do you think it would take you to
learn this perfectly, and by heart?" the former
enquired.

The street musician glanced at the score, and
then looked dubious.

"It's blinkin' 'ard, guv'nor," he said doubtfully.
"I wouldn't reckon to play this in less than a
coupler weeks."

"Splendid," our musician exclaimed. "Take
the music with you, practise it day and night,
and when you're quite perfect let me know. It'll
mean at least half a sovereign for you, and probably
more."

The musician expressed himself willing to do
his best, and two or three weeks later reported
that he could play that particular piece " on me
'ed."

"Very good," said his temporary employer,
"be outside the 'Dog and Duck' at——" he
mentioned the time of an intermission in our
performance when various members of the orchestra
were accustomed to slip out and "have one,"
"and when I give you the signal," he added,
"just let it go for all you're worth. And see "—
in grim warning this—"that you don't make any
mistakes."

The intermission arrived, and our trumpet player
cannot but have been struck with the sudden

increase of his personal popularity, for one and all of his confrères were insistent that he should join them in refreshment. Accordingly they trooped across *en masse* to the " Dog and Duck."

There, drinks were ordered. It was at the exact moment when the talented player was raising his glass to his lips, that from the street immediately outside came the strident but entirely correct rendition of the bars that were his own latest triumph.

In all my life I never saw a look of such utter amazement on the face of any human being as upon his at that moment. The glass dropped from his hand to fall, broken but unheeded, on the floor.

And from the moment the joke was explained his head began quite sensibly to diminish in size. Actually he became one of the most popular members of the orchestra. But he never was permitted to forget that cornet soloist.

The second incident which, as I have said already, occurred also at Covent Garden, saw myself as the victim.

Nicolas Tscherepnine had been engaged to conduct his ballet, the " Romance of a Mummy," which he had written expressly for Pavlova. It so happened it came to her knowledge that the opening night would coincide with the twenty-fifth anniversary of his debut as a composer. Immediately it occurred to her that it would be a graceful tribute to make a small subscription among the company for the purchase of some little memento to mark the occasion, and that, on behalf of the orchestra, I should make the presentation from the stage.

With some knowledge, however, of Nicolas Tscherepnine's effusive temperament, it was my dread that in the excitement of the moment, and according to the Russian manner, he would insist upon kissing me. Foolishly, I mentioned this apprehension to more than one of the company.

" I am determined," I said firmly, " that at all costs I will not let him kiss me. I loathe and detest the practice among men, and furthermore I am not going to be made a fool of in front of a crowded audience like Covent Garden."

They expressed sympathy with my views—the hypocrites !—and there and then proceeded to take dastardly advantage of the opening with which I had been fool enough to present them.

For they went round to Tscherepnine, whom by this time it had become necessary to let into the secret of the forthcoming presentation.

" Don't say anything to Stier," they said warningly, " but between ourselves there is only one way in which you will really be able to convince him of your pleasure."

Not unnaturally the great Russian musician enquired what that was.

" On no account must you omit to kiss him," they urged. " He may pretend to object, but that will only be his diffidence. The more he struggles the more you must insist, and the more he'll like it."

The upshot of that presentation I can convey no more adequately than by reproducing an extract from a contemporary issue of the *Daily Express :*

CONDUCTORS KISS ON THE STAGE

REMARKABLE SCENE AT COVENT GARDEN

Covent Garden, the home of grand opera and classical ballet, witnessed last night a scene which must be almost unprecedented in its annals. Two famous conductors kissed on the stage in full view of a crowded and enthusiastic audience. . . .

Appropriately enough, before the production of " Divertissements " Tscherepnine was led on to the stage by Mr. Theodore Stier, the usual conductor of the Covent Garden orchestra, who made him a presentation on behalf of the orchestra.

Tscherepnine, who seemed filled with emotion at the honour . . . implanted a full kiss on the face of Mr. Stier. Meanwhile the audience applauded rapturously. . . .

It was all very informal, but the audience loved it.

The audience may have loved it, but to the victim, which was myself, it was a moment of intense agony.

It was in Dublin occurred another practical joke, with this time Pavlova herself as instigator and myself as delighted seconder to her efforts.

When the company arrived at the Irish capital in 1912, I discovered that my friend, William Orpen (now Sir William), was teaching painting at the Academy there, and thus I was not surprised to receive a letter from him inviting me to lunch at Jammet's Restaurant on the following day.

Delighted as I was to know that my friend had not forgotten me, the invitation came rather at an awkward time. M. Dandré was away, and it was an understood thing that I took Pavlova to lunch each day. However, with a sound knowledge of her understanding nature I took Orpen's letter to her, and asked her what was the best to be done.

Immediately her face lighted.

"My dear," she said, "we will play a joke on your friend. You will go to him and say that since your arrival in Dublin you have formed an attachment for a young lady resident, and that you cannot lunch with him because actually she is waiting outside the restaurant. Then your Mr. Orpen will say, 'Then, my dear Stier, by all means bring her in.' You will go outside to discover Pavlova, but not for a long time will your Mr. Orpen find out who is his guest; she will be so modest and retiring."

The scheme worked even as she had prophesied. "By all means bring her in, old chap," Orpen said heartily. And I went outside to return with a modestly, indeed almost shabbily, dressed young lady; one, moreover, who was wearing a very thick veil indeed.

For the first two or three courses our guest opened her mouth only to place food in it, and except for that mouth and chin the heavy veil entirely concealed her features. To all the attempts of our host to draw her into the conversation, she returned only the shortest and most demure of

monosyllables. It was not long before I perceived
Orpen casting glances of reproach at me that I
should have inflicted this reunion with the presence
of such a palpable " dumb-bell."

His expression, however, when eventually she
raised her veil and he recognised the angel he had
been entertaining unawares, was alone worth all
the trouble of our hoax. For a moment he gazed
at her speechlessly. Then, irresistibly, he burst
into a great shout of laughter, in which both
Pavlova and myself joined.

The remainder of that luncheon was one of the
cheeriest within my recollection. To commemorate
it, Orpen made a sketch on the menu card, a
reproduction of which faces this page.

I have another memory of Dublin, however, of
an event that took place long before I met Pavlova,
and which is by no means so pleasant as the one
just recounted, for I still wear a scar in the service
of Queen Victoria.

At that time I was a member of a small orchestra
engaged to play at Dublin Castle during the season.
On her last visit to Ireland as the guest at the
Viceregal Lodge in Phœnix Park, Queen Victoria
requested that we should be lent, one evening, for
her entertainment.

It so happened, however, that owing to the
early hour at which the Queen was in the habit
of dining, we were given very short notice of the
honour to be conferred upon us, and in my nervousness I succeeded, while shaving, in inflicting a
gash which necessitated my removal to the Lower

ORPEN'S DREAM—THE DAY AFTER MEETING PAVLOVA

Facing page 220

Bagot Street Hospital, where I had five stitches put in the wound.

Dublin seems not to have been a very fortunate place for Pavlova, either. It was there, on the opening night of the visit which saw Orpen's informal introduction to her, that in the middle of a dance she was knocked down by the collapse of a piece of scenery. And though with customary pluck she crawled from beneath the debris and continued her dance as if nothing had happened, it was only to discover later that her whole body was one mass of bruises.

It was in Ireland, also, that we played to the smallest house within my recollection. At our opening night at Belfast the audience numbered just fourteen people. It is typical of Pavlova, however, that she worked to please that tiny crowd as hard as though she was appearing before thousands.

" It would not be fair to allow those who are here to suffer because others have stayed away," she explained.

Her reward was an enthusiasm from those fourteen people such as never before or since had we played to.

The explanation of the sparse attendance was that the date clashed with a political speech from Mr. Winston Churchill, and the Irish being what they are, it would have taken a greater attraction even than Pavlova to have weaned them from such a demonstration.

Certainly, for the rest of the week, each house was packed to overflowing.

CHAPTER XIV

ONE of the most brilliant personalities with whom I ever came into contact was an Englishman by the name of Arthur Johnston, who, at the time of our first meeting, was teaching philology at Edinburgh. His appearance, too, was in keeping with his talents, for he was strikingly reminiscent of a well-groomed Beethoven.

Johnston was the nearest approach to an Admirable Crichton of modern times it is possible to imagine. In addition to teaching Greek and Latin he spoke, and with hardly a trace of accent, no less than four modern languages : German, French, Spanish, and Russian, the latter acquired during his tutorship in the House of Prince Galitzin.

Besides having written and published essays and poems in German and French, his knowledge of Greek and Latin literature was as extensive as it was thorough. He was a brilliant pianist and composer, and his knowledge of painting and sculpture was only a little less authentic than his knowledge of music. And in addition, of all good things, he was a wonderful amateur conjuror.

In spite of the excellent position he held at Edinburgh, like many other brilliant people he wanted badly to be something different from what actually he was. His particular inclination lay towards becoming the musical critic of the *Manchester Guardian,* a newspaper he was in the habit of describing as the greatest in England.

He achieved his wish eventually, and left Edinburgh to take up the coveted position on the staff of that journal, a niche he filled with such brilliance that even now his contributions are quoted as models in style and structure of what musical criticism should be. It was while he was so engaged that the acquaintance we had formed in Edinburgh developed into one of the closest personal friendships of my life.

Then I left Manchester and for some time lost sight of him. Quite considerably later, while I was enjoying a holiday in Vienna, I was taking my ease in the Café Parsifal, which, as the name suggests, is the favourite rendezvous of conductors and musicians, when the waiter approached with the information: " A Turkish gentleman wishes to speak to you, Sir."

I turned, and to my surprise and no little amusement discovered Arthur Johnston, complete with frock coat and Turkish fez, threading his way between the tables towards me.

He explained that his costume was due to the prevailing trouble in Crete, to where—a tribute to his versatility as the only member of the staff with a knowledge of Greek—he had been despatched as Special Correspondent by his paper.

He had taken Vienna on his way home with the sole object of finding me, his call at the Café Parsifal being for that purpose. Actually his idea was to

get in touch with Dr. Hans Richter, an introduction
he relied upon me to effect. As the great conductor
was an habitué of the Café, and I was very well
known to him, there was no difficulty about this.
So far as my memory serves I was able to bring
the two together that same day.

Richter was not without his peculiarities; by
no means was he all things to all men. Fortunately,
as I had but little doubt would be the case, he took
to Arthur Johnston immediately. And during that
first interview transpired the underlying motive
for Arthur Johnston's presence in Vienna. It
was to sound Richter as to his willingness to consider coming to Manchester as Director of the
Hallé Orchestra. The direct outcome of the interview I had the privilege of arranging, then, was
the initiation of negotiations which led to Richter
fulfilling that position for a period of three years.

Poor Arthur Johnston died at the early age of
about forty-five, a tragedy that was a greater loss
to British art and musical criticism than has yet
been realised.

It was in a very remarkable way that I was
brought into contact with another unique and
brilliant personality. In the early days of my
emigration to this country the orchestra to which
I was attached in Glasgow used occasionally to
play in Paisley. There it was an understood thing
that I stayed at the house of the Mayor, from
whom, as from his charming and cultured wife,
I received the most kind and open-hearted hospitality. Every time an engagement was arranged

in Paisley I used to advise them, and always their carriage would meet me at the station to drive me straight to their beautiful house.

On one of the tables in the drawing-room was the photograph of a man in clerical dress whose face was so strikingly handsome and æsthetic that it could not but engage the attention of anyone with any pretence of being a judge of character.

The Mayoress told me that the original was the Minister of the Presbyterian Church attended by the family, and that in addition he was a very close personal friend. She was good enough to add, also, that she was most anxious that we should meet. For some reason, however, she was never able to bring this about, so that I left Scotland at last with the introduction still uneffected.

It was no less than twenty-seven years later, while travelling on the *Finland* from America, that I noticed in the smoke-room a gentleman of extremely striking personality whose face seemed vaguely familiar. Yet, puzzle as I might, for the life of me I could not place him, and for two or three days we exchanged glances of mute enquiry. Then, in a flash of illumination, suddenly I remembered. Unless I was very greatly mistaken, allowing for the difference of twenty-seven years, he was the original of the photograph in which I had been so interested in the drawing-room of the Mayoress of Paisley.

Immediately I went over to him.

" My name is Theodore Stier," I said. " Is it

P

possible that I am speaking to the Reverend Hugh Black ? "

Even before he spoke it was obvious from his expression that he recognised my name, for his face lighted with comprehension.

" Surely you are not the Mr. Stier who was so great a friend of my own friends in Paisley," he exclaimed, " and of whom I heard so much ? "

From that moment we spent most of our waking hours together, and during our many long and delightful talks he told me that he had left Scotland to take up the chair of Professor of Theology at Columbia University in New York, a position he had filled, at the time of which I write, for many years.

I do not ever remember a man whose conversation was more wholly engrossing than that of Professor Hugh Black. He was less clouded by the flesh than I could have thought it possible for any human mind to achieve. Spiritually he seemed to be washed clear of any taint of materialism; dowered with a true sense of values which made of his life a very lovely thing. He absorbed and fascinated me to such an extent at last that I was led to apologise for taking up so much of his time. He must have other things to do, I pointed out, than walk about the deck talking to me.

He smiled, and said that beyond one or two letters it was necessary to answer, he had no preoccupation of any kind. I said, then, that I would read for an hour or so, and thus enable him to get through his correspondence.

And this is where the amazing coincidence comes in.

I went into the ship's library and picked out the first book that came to my hand, which happened to be Lord Fisher's Reminiscences. I opened it haphazard, and the very first name that struck my eyes was that of Professor Hugh Black.

Here is the extract I read, and which occurs on page 77.

" I have been sitting this morning under a Presbyterian minister, Dr. Hugh Black, whose eloquence so moved the Prime Minister, Mr. Lloyd George (who kindly gave me a seat in his pew, on the other side of me being President Wilson . . .), that the moment the service was over the Prime Minister went straight to him in the pulpit and told him it was one of the best sermons he had ever heard, and it probably was."

Going back to Richter, my own memories of him are particularly vivid by reason of the time I was a member of his London orchestra. And what an autocrat he was ! His method of obtaining efficiency was discipline carried to the point of terrorism. The tiniest mistake would call forth a torrent of vituperation calculated to reduce the offender to a state of nervous collapse. Actually I have known a musician crawl under the seat of a railway carriage in the hope of escaping retribution for some trivial musical misdemeanour.

At the time of my Vienna visit the most famous Austrian musical critic was Hanslick.

There is a story of him being sent to Bayreuth

to report on the performance of "Parsifal." At the theatre he found himself seated next to a venerable old gentleman who, in the course of conversation, displayed a knowledge of the score that quite astonished Hanslick by its penetration—especially as at that time "Parsifal" had not long been written. After the performance Hanslick made a point of accompanying the old gentleman to the station to see him off by train, and only then thought it necessary to divulge his name. The old gentleman beamed.

"I knew all the time it was my privilege to converse with a great man," he said delightedly. And then, just as the train was on the point of pulling out, added: "You must allow me to give you my card."

When the train had disappeared, Hanslick glanced at the pasteboard in his hand, to read:

"Don Pedro, Emperor of Brazil."

Harping back to those musical conductors whose methods are calculated to inspire awe, I have a very vivid recollection of Toscanini, who, in my opinion, is the greatest living Italian conductor.

Apart from his masterful methods, his memory of a score is simply uncanny. I remember him receiving a copy of Puccini's "The Girl from the Golden West" one Monday morning, and conducting the whole of the first act from memory on the following Thursday. Also, entirely without a score, I have known him to conduct three operas in one week at the Opera House in New York, "Valkyrie," "Tristan," and "Alcesti."

It is unfortunate that his control of the orchestra

did not extend to a similar discipline of his own temper, which was ungovernable. It is said that upon one occasion in Italy he threw his baton at a violinist with such force that, striking the musician's bow, it caused the point to penetrate his eye so violently that the injured member had to be removed, an accident which, so the story goes, gave rise to what I should imagine is the most remarkable legal decision in musical history. For when the violinist sued Toscanini in the Courts for damage, the irascible conductor got off scot free, the magistrate holding gravely that no genius is responsible for his actions !

Another conductor with methods somewhat similar to Toscanini was the German, Scheel, who by methods of belittlement and abuse had his orchestra reduced to a state of trembling subjection. But there was one occasion, at least, when to the ill-concealed delight of everybody present, he rather more than met his match.

It happened in Philadelphia that the solo 'cellist failed to grasp the torrent of instructions Scheel hurled at him. This so infuriated the conductor that he descended to personalities. Finally, he said that which no American could pass without active protest. The protest of the 'cellist took very practical form.

Very slowly and deliberately he leaned his instrument against his chair. Then, still without the least haste, he produced his watch from his waistcoat pocket, and from his hip a large and businesslike revolver.

" Say, Mr. Conductor," he drawled slowly, " I'll give you just five minutes to take back those words. If at the end of that time you haven't done so, why, I'll shoot you like the mad dog you are."

Retaining his seat only with difficulty the terrified Scheel began to mumble incoherent protest, a demonstration to which the 'cellist's sole reply was audibly to tick off the half-minutes from his watch. But long before the arrival of the tenth of these periods the conductor had abjectly climbed down.

His apology, indeed, was fulsome in the extreme. And then, and only then, the rehearsal was allowed to proceed.

But how different were the methods of Sir George Henschel, to whose kindly consideration I referred in telling of his insistence, upon my first meeting with him in Glasgow, that I should wear warmer underclothing. This small incident was only typical of the sympathy and understanding he brought to bear upon all the orchestral musicians who came under his direction.

Sir Henry J. Wood is another conductor who combines kindness and sympathy with a firmness which engages the respect of his orchestras. A typical example of his sympathy occurred some three years after I joined him. Happening to meet him casually in the street, he asked me what future I had mapped out for myself. I told him that it was my ambition to become a conductor.

Sir Henry laid his hand very earnestly on my arm.

" My dear young man," he said, " if you really feel that it is your *métier*, let no one in the world discourage you from fulfilling it. It will be a struggle, as no one knows better than myself, for I had to fight very hard, indeed, for my position. But I stuck to my ambition, and you must do the same."

If men who have reached the heights could realise what a word of sympathy may mean to those on the lower rungs of the ladder, they would, I think, be a little less chary with their encouragement. I know that with those kindly words of Sir Henry's in my mind, and in my heart, I walked home that day on air.

One of the greatest, but unfortunately one of the most torrential, conductors under whom I served, was Gustav Mahler, who at that time controlled the Opera House at Hamburg, and who, it is not too much to say, was unpopular with stage and orchestra alike. I remember once while a cholera scare was in progress, and he failed to turn up at the usual time, a message came through to say that he was ill. The rumour spread that he had fallen a victim to the epidemic. Immediately, and spontaneously, the orchestra struck up one of the liveliest of Strauss's valses as a song of thanksgiving, and for the rest of that day the prevailing atmosphere was one of unusual cheerfulness. It was not until the next morning, when, very much alive, and more brusque and hostile than ever, he was found in his customary place, that once more gloom descended upon the Hamburg Opera House.

With those other cantankerous directors of whom I have written, there were at least gradations in their ill-temper according to the position of those upon whom they vented it. With Mahler there was no such discrimination ; he was as severe with the *prima donna* as with his last fiddle.

Toward the end of the season it seemed gradually to dawn upon him that for some obscure reason he was not as greatly beloved as his merits as a musician so justly warranted.

Could the reason for this be, he appeared to ask himself, that there had been occasions when the natural stupidity of all with whom he had been called upon to deal had led him to depart, however slightly, from the meticulous courtesy of demeanour which was his habit ? If so, this must instantly be put right.

So he invited the whole orchestra to dinner, and at the end made a brief speech in which with obvious sincerity he expressed regret for anything he may have said from time to time that had hurt the feelings of any of those under his baton.

But it was too late. He discovered that although those present were content to eat his food, not one was brave enough to stand up to propose his health. At last the awkwardness and constraint became such that, under the plea of being the baby of the company, I rose hesitantly to my feet, and in the most inept and tactless speech of my career, attempted to say something adequate to the occasion.

The success of my efforts may be judged from

the fact that while seven of the orchestra rose to
drink Mahler's health, no less than seventy-three
remained silent and sullen in their seats And
immediately afterwards I was advised to flee from
the wrath to come in the form of an infuriated
orchestra hunting my blood for the offence of
daring to propose the health of Gustav Mahler.
Nevertheless, I thought then, as I think now, that
had we understood him better relations might not
have been so strained. And to a conductor with
the genius of Mahler, and one whose devotion to
his art was so whole-souled, much may be forgiven.

What a contrast to Mahler was Nikisch, under
whom I played in London. In no orchestra with
which I have been associated were relations more
delightful. There was not a musician under his
control who was not devoted to Nikisch by reason
of the entirely natural attitude with which he
accepted them simply as fellow-artists, and because
he made no attempt to rule, but only to lead, his
reward was full and immediate from every single
member of the orchestra, not one of whom was
ever known to suggest leaving rehearsal until the
desired end had been achieved. And so it was that
just as I never remember seeing a member of his
orchestra glance anxiously at his watch, so I do
not remember Nikisch ever losing his temper.

Pavlova's most famous Ballet Masters have been
Michael Fokine, Ivan Clustine, Alexander Schirajeff,
and Peter Zailich, who was the youngest of them
all, and who composed the dances for Strauss's

" Valse Printemps " and " Popular Pastorale," in the latter of which Muriel Stewart so excelled.

But for the War, Zailich undoubtedly would have risen to a great height in his profession. At the outbreak of hostilities he was with the company in Germany, but managed to escape official vigilance and return to Russia. His regiment was one of the first to be sent to the front, and in the very first engagement Zailich was captured, and sent to Germany as a prisoner of war. Here, over a considerable period, he had a very bad time indeed.

Suddenly, an idea came to him. He wrote a petition to the High Command in which he informed authority that it was only a month or two previously he had been the principal male dancer at the Gala Performance in honour of the birth of an heir to the House of Brunswick, at which the Kaiser himself had been present, and suggested that this warranted a mitigation of his lot. It is satisfactory to relate, moreover, that his plea was justified in its result, for from thence forward Zailich had a very much easier time than fell to the lot of the majority of war prisoners in Germany.

But while Zailich was distinguished for his progressiveness, Schirajeff was definitely reactionary and anti-modernist ; entirely content to pass on the great Moscow tradition that was founded by old Petita, the father of the Russian ballet. Above all things he hated with particular ferocity all tendencies to effeminate or exaggerated movements of the arms and body.

" Dancing is dancing," he would exclaim emphatically, " and it is the feet that have to do it."

He it was who was responsible for the Hornpipe Dance, in which he performed so incomparably, and for the choreography of Drice's " The Magic Flute," and the very delightful humorous ballet, " La Fille Mel Gardee." In spite of his prejudices and slightly exaggerated mannerisms, Schirajeff was loved by every one for his affectionate nature, general kind-heartedness, and exceptionally keen sense of humour.

The most fascinating of this quartette of Ballet Masters, however, was Fokine. It was one of his peculiarities that he refused consistently to prepare his compositions beforehand, preferring to think them out from bar to bar as he went along. His method was to have a phrase played to him. Then he would put his head into his hands and remain entirely motionless, sometimes for as long as half an hour at a time, until seized by the necessary inspiration.

He was helped greatly in his work by a very exact knowledge of literature both ancient and modern, erudition he combined with a command of music which enabled him to treat the intention of the composer with reverent understanding. Also, he could work out the counterpoint with such exactitude that, just as the music could bring out two melodies at the same time, so he could keep two dances going simultaneously. It was he who composed for Madame Pavlova the celebrated " Dying Swan " and Rubenstein's " Valse Caprice."

Perhaps the most popular male principal we ever had in the company was Novikoff, that patient and hard-working artist who, whatever the conditions or hardships, was never once known to utter a word of complaint.

In private life he conveys the impression of being shy, ascetic, and with the weight of all the troubles of the world on his shoulders—a strange contrast to his bearing on the stage.

For then at once he is the muscular giant, a man of perfect development, the envy of professional wrestlers. And apart from his bodily perfection, both in his artistic and private life he is the very incarnation of sincerity, being essentially of the type to whom sorrow brings only a greater understanding; it may be, indeed, that some part at least of this fineness of spirit was brought about by his experiences in the Russian Revolution. Before that holocaust he had contrived to save a very considerable portion, every penny of which was taken from him, and after an eight months' journey, during which there were periods when he was forced to live by dancing in beer gardens, he arrived in London a penniless refugee.

From the technical standpoint of neatness and facility Volinine was the most nimble of Pavlova's partners, though in artistry and manliness he was not to be compared with Novikoff, nor, indeed, with Mordkin   Where Volinine particularly shone, however, was in the precision of his dancing.

I have mentioned previously, I think, his rather casual habits in private life. As the son of a wealthy merchant in Moscow his early training had left him a little spoilt and finicky in his everyday requirements. He was one of those men who want what they want when they want it. One rather amusing instance of this peculiarity, and in which, incidentally, he rather more than met his màtch, happened while he was staying in a large and ornate hotel in South America.

If by Bohemian is meant one who refuses to be bound by conventions to which the majority subscribe, then Volinine was a Bohemian of the Bohemians. One demonstration of this was that he emphatically declined to be bound down to any set hour for meals.

In this particular hotel it was a matter of grievance that he had some difficulty in being served with breakfast at one o'clock in the afternoon, and lunch at five. On the day in question, having ordered his first meal well after the noon hour had struck, and waited in vain some forty-five minutes for its arrival, his indignation got the better of him. At one o'clock to the stroke he leapt out of bed and descended tempestuously to give the matter his personal attention.

That particular hotel happened to be the luncheon rendezvous for all the wealthy and fashionable of the town, who, at one o'clock precisely, were accustomed to crowd the vestibule, gossiping and sipping cocktails before adjourning to the restaurant. On this particular day, then, the elevator came to an abrupt stop in their midst, the gates were flung open, and through the silken ranks of fashion dashed a dishevelled gesticulating and pyjama-clad Volinine, clamouring at the top of his voice to be informed why the ―――― he hadn't been served with breakfast !

It is a tribute to the *savoir-faire* of the manager that, whatever his real feelings, at least he retained his poise, for it was without any comment whatever he listened to Volinine's tirade. When the explosion had died down sufficiently for him to gain a hearing, he said :

" Quite obviously, sir, this hotel is not to your liking. Hence it would be better for you to try another. I will have your luggage sent down―at once."

And it was even so.

But in spite of his eccentricities and quick out-bursts of temper, Volinine was large-hearted and generous-minded. For is it not told of him that, being a member of a company of artists stranded in an American town, he paid all the bills of the *corps de ballet* and bought their tickets to New York.

Another outstanding personality in the company was Butsova, whose parents kept a sweet shop in Nottingham. Though she was only fourteen when she joined us at Bristol, it was not long before it became apparent that she was possessed of quite extraordinary talent. Besides being pretty and graceful, I do not remember any girl to whom dancing came more easily. Pavlova was of the opinion―and it is one which even my own limited knowledge enables me to share―that had Butsova possessed greater powers of concentration there are no heights to which she might not legitimately have aspired in her profession. With these qualities somewhat lacking, however, she soon lost patience, and in 1925 severed her connection with the company to accept an engagement in America.

One of my vividest recollections in connection with Butsova is of the characteristic consideration with which, whenever the company were playing in Nottingham, Pavlova would alter the programme in order to allow the local girl the greatest possible scope.

Upon one of our tours a Russian dancer was engaged to take the place of one of the principals who had fallen ill, and arrived complete with husband. This man, a Swede, who from that time travelled with the company, was one of the most extraordinary characters with whom the Pavlova Company was ever connected. Quite frankly he was not quite *compis mentis*.

His peculiarity took the form of a not unusual form of religious mania. With his pockets stuffed with Bibles, it was his aim to convert to his own idea of salvation everyone with whom he came into contact.

It was unfortunate for him that one of his first subjects should have been the highly temperamental Volinine, an error in psychology which took place in the smoking-room of the ship. I do not know what Volinine's ideas of religion are, though from my knowledge of him I should judge them to be somewhat embryonic. In any case they were not to be influenced by a semi-witted Swede, however earnest and insistent.

As might have been anticipated the result was unfortunate, the Swede upbraiding the Russian as the blackest of black sheep, Volinine retaliating by presenting the evangelist with the blackest of black eyes.

Like so many of those unfortunates who labour under mental disability, this religious fervour of our friend was not his only obsession. He was under the firm idea that as well as having a large staff of missionaries—his " soldiers " he called them—he possessed almost unlimited influence with Government circles at Washington. Hence it was that whenever anything, of however trivial a nature, occurred to offend him, his brow would darken and with a threatening scowl he would mutter menacingly :

" You wait ! Washington shall hear about this ! And "—said with intense significance—" I have my soldiers working for me."

Whether it was the quality of the food served in his hotel, of which he complained, or if, as was not infrequent, he was annoyed that his wife did not receive the same amount of attention as Pavlova, his threat was always the same, Washington should hear of it.

" In the dressing-room of Madame Pavlova the carpet is more thick, more new, than in the dressing-room of my wife," he would complain bitterly. Or, " You, Maestro, do you not conduct, oh, so much more eloquently for Madame than for

A RARE PHOTOGRAPH OF PAVLOVA

my wife ? But "—with infinite menace—" wait.
Washington shall hear of it ! "

I remember that once, travelling by train, he
entered into a conversation with some nuns who
were *en route* to a neighbouring town. When
questioned good-naturedly as to the subject of their
conversation he explained gravely that the religious
devotees in question were some of his " soldiers."

Another delusion, not unusual, I believe, with
those who are not " quite bright," was that he
was continually spied upon by enemies in quest
of his destruction.

It was, I suppose, inevitable that there should
be times when this peculiarity was played upon to
provide entertainment for the rest of the company.
Travelling from Vancouver to Victoria upon one
occasion, we were fellow-passengers with a pale-
faced, rather impressive-looking gentleman, with
a long black beard, who to be truthful was not
unlike the stage conception of a conspirator. This
individual, our Swedish friend complained, was
looking at him very much more intently than he
could quite understand the reason for.

With the opening thus gratuitously presented, it
was not long before one or two of the younger
members of the company approached the black-
bearded conspirator, who in real life, incidentally,
was a Vancouver hairdresser, and letting him into
the secret of our Swedish friend's peculiarity, persuaded him to follow the latter about wherever
he went, and, when he could catch his victim's eye,
to stare intently and furiously into his face.

Q

The result exceeded all expectations. It so happened, that during a discussion on the immigration laws of various countries, which had taken place on the ship, it had been stated how particular the Canadian authorities were as to the moral integrity of those they permitted to enter the country, and that, following this discussion, our Swedish friend had been noticed to be overcome with slight depression of spirit. I cannot write as to its truth, but there was an impression current that in spite of his evangelistic prepossession, the union of the Swede and his lady had not yet been blessed either by Church or State. Be that as it may, the Vancouver hairdresser was indicated by his persecutors as a detective appointed by the Canadian Government for the express purpose of investigating the eligibility of the parties to remain in the country.

Speaking broadly, I should say that if the Swede was hovering on the brink of mental affliction, his experiences of that night were calculated to turn the scale. Hour after hour he spent in a ceaseless patrol of the various alley-ways, a vigil that was punctuated by call after call upon the various cabins wherein slept—or tried to—the male members of the company, for the purpose of imploring their aid and protection against the fiend who so ruthlessly was determined to track him to his doom!

His only consolation was that, in due time, Washington should hear about it!

CHAPTER XV

IN the early stages of my career I belonged to a small Drawing-room Orchestra. In this capacity, from 1899 to 1904, it was my privilege for two months in each season to play at Sandringham during the residence of the late King Edward and Queen Alexandra.

I hardly need state that this was a period to which I used to look forward very keenly. As most people know, King Edward was a great lover of music. Also, he was very considerate in his treatment of the orchestra. Actually our duties were extremely light, entailing only playing from 9.15 until 11 o'clock each evening, at which latter hour Queen Alexandra would rise from her seat as a signal that the concert was at an end. It was towards the end of one of these occasions occurred the only time I ever saw King Edward annoyed.

At five minutes to eleven one night he instructed us to play his favourite selection, the " Meister-singers." This put us in somewhat of a quandary. The concert was supposed to close at eleven, and here we had a demand for a selection which in its normal arrangement would occupy about thirty-five minutes. Hence the conductor thought it better, by making a judicious cut, to bring the time down to seven or eight minutes.

243

But that did not in the least suit His Majesty, for when, the moment the last bar had been played, he rose from his seat, it was not difficult to perceive his displeasure.

"What exactly do you mean by that ? " he said coldly. "Where was the quintette ? Where was Pogner's address ? Where was Beckmesser's Serenade ? Absolute laziness, I call it." He paused, and then added : "And now for a punishment you will play over the whole selection. From beginning to end, please."

It was in my hearing, and in connection with this same selection of the " Meistersingers," that King Edward rebuked a very high dignitary of the Church.

The two were alone in the room with us as it was being played. His face alive with pleasure, the King indicated to his companion each melody as it was given. "That is the so-and-so," he would say. Or : "Now we are coming to Beckmesser's Serenade."

To His Majesty's obvious surprise, however, and beyond polite gestures of acquiescence, the clergyman appeared somewhat unresponsive. When the selection was finished, then, King Edward turned to him.

"What is your opinion of the 'Meistersingers'?" he enquired. "Personally, it is my favourite opera."

The great Churchman admitted diffidently that he knew nothing whatever about it, a statement at which King Edward's astonishment was evident in his expression.

" Not know the ' Meistersingers ' ! Is it possible ! " he exclaimed.

His companion owned that, to his great regret, he had hitherto missed hearing it.

" Then," said His Majesty emphatically, " you have missed one of the greatest marvels that humanity has yet succeeded in achieving."

On the night of the arrival of the telegram which announced the severe repulse of the British Army at Magersfontein, Mr. (now Lord) Balfour and Joseph Chamberlain were standing behind Queen Alexandra—at that time Princess of Wales—who was playing whist. At one stage of the game Chamberlain leaned forward and observed respectfully :

" I'm afraid, Ma'am, you won't win this game."

The Princess looked up with a very grave smile.

" Nevertheless, I hope devoutly that you will win yours," she said quietly.

In sending out the invitations to the Christmas parties at Sandringham, it was the custom for each card to contain a number which corresponded with one upon the present that had been chosen for the guest. In distributing the gifts, however, Queen Alexandra entirely disregarded this. With the jolliest smile imaginable she would approach a guest.

" Now, what would you like ? " she would ask kindly. " Never mind the silly old number, please have something you really want."

On one occasion she came to me with a lady's purse in her hand.

" This," she said graciously, " is just the very thing for your wife."

" But, Ma'am," I protested, " unfortunately I have no wife."

" Then," said the Queen promptly, " it will do for your sweetheart. Don't dare to tell me you haven't a sweetheart."

And that is why to-day within the archives where are enshrined those one or two momentoes of more than usually happy association is included a little purse that was selected especially by a Royal Princess for that other princess who, alas, so far my roving life has failed to materialise.

Invariably in those Sandringham house parties would be included some great personality in the world of Art or Letters.

One year I remember it was Sir Arthur Sullivan, whose reply, to a lady who was speaking to him on the fame the years had brought him, and of the material joys this success must inevitably have carried in its train, remains poignantly in my recollection. Quite unmoved, apparently, by the tribute, Sir Arthur listened in silence to all she had to say. Then he looked at her rather grimly.

" Quite so," he assented quietly. To add: " Particularly as my Doctor has just told me that unless I keep strictly to a diet of rusks and soda water I have just six months to live." Then the gloom cleared from his face, replaced by an impish smile. " But watch me at dinner to-night," he exclaimed gaily. " A short life and a merry one is my motto ! "

Queen Alexandra, at least, was not in the habit of regarding either her gains or losses at the card table with any degree of seriousness. I remember that one night, playing against the King of Spain, the run of the cards was so phenomenally against her that His Majesty was moved to condolence.

Unfortunately, however, at that time his English was not so fluent as afterwards it became. He turned to his Ambassador and enquired :

" How would you say : ' No se ocupe por tiempo de mala suerte, que sin duda cambiará en un momento á otro y despues Ud. tendra constantemente manos buenas y entonces sera muestro tiempo de grunir ' ? "

To which the Ambassador answered with a smile :

" I should just say, ' Cheer up.' "

Actually these card games were never treated very seriously. One night Queen Alexandra, Princess Victoria, Queen Amelie of Portugal, and another lady, becoming somewhat tired of waiting for the gentlemen, who were sitting rather long over their port, commenced a game of bridge. It was a more than usually pleasant house party that year, with everyone in high spirits as a consequence. Thus it was not long before the game became more in the nature of a frolic than a serious effort, the cards falling continually to the floor. The result was that King Edward entered the room to discover the Queen of Portugal under the table, groping for the cards. As she became aware of

His Majesty's presence, she popped up her head and, hardly able to control her laughter, pointed at Queen Alexandra.

" Elle triche tous les temps ! " she exclaimed, laughing heartily.

One of the most ludicrous incidents I remember was one night when the Duke of Portland came hurrying into the room where we were awaiting the arrival of the Royal party, shouting excitedly :

" Queenie ! Queenie ! Queenie ! "

Under the impression that he was announcing the imminent approach of Her Majesty, we sprang instantly to our feet and struck up the National Anthem !

Queenie, I might mention, was his Grace's favourite terrier !

On the respective birthdays of the King and Queen the usual musical programme was set aside and a special one arranged, the ballroom being turned into a concert room for the occasion, and special artists brought down from London.

I remember that at one of these performances the principal attraction was a very prominent conjurer and illusionist whose name it is not necessary to mention. Gifted as he was, the early education of this particular performer had been somewhat neglected, so that however intensively he had been schooled beforehand as to the etiquette necessary to preserve before Royalty, it soon became apparent his lesson had not penetrated as deeply as could have been wished.

One part of his performance had to deal with

card tricks. Stepping from the platform he approached Queen Alexandra, who was seated in the front row of the chairs, and very respectfully asked Her Majesty to choose a card from the pack in his hand, make a mental note of it, and put it back into the pack, which very graciously she did.

"What card was it, your Majesty?" he later enquired.

The Queen informed him that it was the seven of clubs.

And then, in his best showman's manner, the conjurer exclaimed at the top of his voice:

"Now that *was* clever of you. You must have got up very early this morning!"

The tense moment which followed was relieved, at last, by a roar of laughter from King Edward, and thus the situation was saved.

But apart from his somewhat unfortunate manner there was no doubt as to the genius of this particular conjurer. There was one trick he performed that evening, I remember, at which no one present was more mystified than our present King, then the Prince of Wales. The performer produced a sack which he displayed to the audience as quite empty. Into this sack, and from a distance of some inches from its mouth, he dropped an egg. When, holding the sack at its extreme edges by only the tips of his fingers, he turned it upside down, no egg emerged, and when he turned the sack inside out, it was empty.

The illusion seemed particularly to impress our

present King, who requested that it might be repeated.

For a moment the conjurer appeared to demur. Eventually, however, he gave way.

" Although it is against the custom of my profession to repeat a trick," he said, " in view of His Royal Highness's request I shall have great pleasure in doing so."

But this second time, in the act of placing the egg in the sack, it was as though the performer made a surreptitious movement towards the breast pocket of his coat. This movement his Royal Highness was quick to detect; equally quick, also, in indicating what he had observed to the conjuror, who appeared overcome with confusion.

At last, as if to make the best of an awkward situation, he asked permission to remove his coat, and this being granted, handed it to the Prince of Wales.

" Perhaps your Royal Highness would be pleased to satisfy yourself that actually the egg *is* in the pocket," he said.

The Prince took the coat, examined it carefully, slipped his hand into the breast pocket, and then, in succession, into the side pockets. The egg was not there.

" Perhaps," the conjurer said, pointing to Lord Lansdowne, " that gentleman might be more fortunate."

Accordingly the coat was passed along, Lord Lansdowne plunged his hand into the breast pocket—and drew out an egg.

" Will you be good enough to replace it in the pocket, and pass the coat back to his Royal Highness," suggested the conjurer, who, incidentally, had remained all the time on the platform and thus was not within several feet of the audience.

Lord Lansdowne handed the coat back to our present King, who for the second time searched the pockets, only to discover them to be empty !

Of course I do not pretend to know how the trick was accomplished. All I can say is that the most amused of those present was the father of the Royal victim of the illusion, King Edward.

Upon one occasion while we were at Sandringham our 'cellist fell ill, and was ordered at once to bed, an occurrence which we regarded as far more unfortunate for him than for ourselves.

As may be imagined there was great competition among musicians for the honour of playing before the Royal house party, and we knew that we had only to hold up a finger to get as many instrumentalists as we wanted. Thus, after we had sent a wire to London for a substitute, we hardly gave the matter a second thought.

We were given very furiously to think later, however, when ten minutes before we were timed to begin no 'cellist had put in an appearance.

With a large orchestra the absence of one instrumentalist is not a very serious matter ; with one as small as ours the absence of a 'cellist would render it impossible to carry on.

While we were feeling most disconcerted, who should pass through the room but Mr. Spencer, the resident detective to whom was entrusted the personal safety of their Majesties—a very cheery fellow, with whom we were all on the friendliest terms. Also, which is rather important to remember, we were all known intimately by sight to each one of his staff.

" What are you all looking so glum about ? " he asked.

" Because," I explained, " our 'cellist is ill in bed, and the substitute we wired for has not yet shown up. Unless he comes we simply can't play."

Just for a moment Spencer looked very concerned for our dilemma. Then suddenly a look of intense consternation appeared in his face, and he drew a horror-stricken hand across his forehead.

" Great Scott ! " he shouted, " I wonder if that's the chap I locked up."

Poor Spencer wasn't to blame ; he had only taken the most elementary precautions for the safety of his Royal charges.

What actually had happened was that the 'cellist, a rather saturnine-looking foreigner with hardly a word of English in his vocabulary, had arrived, complete with suit-case and 'cello, at Dersingham Station.

Finding no conveyance to meet him, he had left his bag and instrument in the cloakroom, and set out on the twenty minutes' walk to Sandringham.

Arrived at the entrance gates, he had not been at all sure that actually he had reached his destination, or if he had, that this was the point at which he would be required to enter the grounds. In his five minutes' rather furtive peerings through the gates in order to determine the question, he had been pounced upon by a policeman, who had been watching these rather suspicious proceedings with growing interest, and told to give an account of himself.

The fact of his suspect's rather sinister appearance, combined with the fact that the only reply he was able to obtain consisted of incoherent mutterings in a strange tongue, had determined the policeman that here was one whose antecedents and motives required quick and searching investigation. If the foreigner had carried his 'cello it might have been different. As it was he was marched straight to Mr. Spencer, who, being able to make nothing of the man's protests, had taken the precaution of locking him up, " pending enquiries."

Once satisfied as to his *bona fides*, of course Spencer at once released him. A pony cart was dispatched to Dersingham for his luggage and instrument, and the concert proceeded as usual.

It was a long time, however, before we allowed the unfortunate 'cellist to forget the reception that was accorded him on his first appearance at Sandringham.

CHAPTER XVI

THE inception of a partnership which contributed more to the art of the drama than any theatrical regime since that of Henry Irving and Ellen Terry at the Lyceum, commenced at the Court Theatre in February of the year 1904 and lasted until June 1907. Nor do I think that in the whole history of the theatre there ever was a coterie of artists banded together with greater loyalty and enthusiasm than the little group of players under the Vedrenne-Barker banner.

The majority of these actors and actresses were then at the beginning of their careers. What they have since become may be read from the programmes of the West End Theatres to-day.

As are so many great beginnings, the inception of the Vedrenne-Barker partnership came very simply into being. At that time the Court Theatre was in the hands of Mr. J. H. Leigh, who was engaged in a series of Shakespearian revivals, besides lecturing on Shakespeare and Shakespearian subjects. J. H. Vedrenne was his manager.

Wishing to produce "The Two Gentlemen of Verona," Vedrenne sent for Granville Barker, who at that time was connected with the Stage Society, and asked his assistance, to which Barker's reply was that he would consent to undertake the production subject to Vedrenne agreeing to stage six matinees of " Candida "—" a play by a friend of mine named Shaw."

Thus was the association founded, an enterprise of which the only recent parallel in aim is to be found in M. Antoine's rule over the Theatre Libre, in Paris, in 1887.

A little later, and quite casually, I was approached with the offer of a guinea per performance to act in the capacity of Musical Director under the new regime—rather a rise in the world, this, from the 6s. 8d. I had once received as deputy for an absent member of the same theatre orchestra.

The first performance I conducted at the Court was something in the nature of an undertaking. It was Granville Barker and Lawrence Housman's " Prunella," a play in which the music was written to fit the rhythm of the verse, so that I had to keep my eyes fixed irrevocably on the mouths of the speakers in order to ensure exact synchronisation.

As I was climbing the stairs to my eyrie at the top of the building the following morning, Vedrenne intercepted me at the door of his office.

" You did quite well yesterday," he said. " And now I suppose you would like a contract ? " He smiled rather grimly. " Not that a contract means anything," he added, " because I've never yet seen one that couldn't be wriggled out of if one of the parties wanted to. Still, I suppose you'd feel more comfortable with a written agreement. How long shall I make the contract for ? "

Although I knew that Vedrenne's word was as binding as anything that could be put in writing, there remained still the chance that it might not always be with him I should have to deal. So very quickly I replied :

" Make it for three years, please."

As I left the theatre that day I was happier than I ever remember to have been before. Human psychology works strangely, and my relief was not so much that for three long years my future was assured as that for the whole of that time I should be relieved of the necessity of carrying my fiddle about with me.

Passing down Bond Street a few days later came my second thrill. Outside Keith Prowse's was displayed a bill of the Court Theatre, and upon it, in modest type, was inscribed my own name as Musical Director.

If I stood in front of that poster for a minute I must have done so for a full quarter of an hour. Even when I tore myself away at last, I had to go back to it to spend another five minutes drinking in the wonderful announcement. I do not suppose that ever again in my life I shall experience quite the same thrill as when upon that day, and for the first time, I saw printed my own name as Musical Director of a first-class London theatre.

One of my first tasks was to rearrange the scores of Brahms and Beethoven. A sinful business this, but one rendered necessary by the smallness of my orchestra. And whatever may have been my diffidence in undertaking this amputation,

this was removed through something Vedrenne
said to me a little later, though actually his words
went only to explain a phenomenon which already
had been brought to my notice—that a large
proportion of the audience had contracted the habit
of remaining in their seats during the orchestral
selection in the intervals.

Vedrenne said : " It's all very well the newspapers saying all sorts of nice things about you,
Stier, but what about Platt (the box-office manager),
who complains that the bar receipts are down
twenty pounds a week through people preferring
to listen to your music than to drink his whisky
and soda ! "

His mention of the Press referred to articles in
the *Daily Telegraph,* in which the writer complained
of the ineptitude of the great majority of London
theatre orchestras, a philippic in which I was
referred to as " that gay young enthusiast Theodore
Stier as the happy exception."

Those were golden days at the Court Theatre, a
time of artistic endeavour carried out under conditions which render it unlikely that a similar
success could be repeated to-day. For if I remember
rightly the Vedrenne-Barker management was in-
augurated on a capital of some five hundred pounds.

But what did that matter to the band of brothers
who laboured so earnestly and with such intense
enthusiasm for the desired end ? Everyone was
too young in years and too fully charged with
optimism even to contemplate failure. Nor, casting
my mind back over the years to a review of those

B

who from time to time were brought into the alliance, can I wonder that the regime constituted such a significant milestone in the history of British theatrical art. Here are some names taken from memory of those who during these two and a half years walked the stage of the Court Theatre :

Dorothy Minto, Edmund Gwenn, Matheson Lang, Lewis Casson, Auriol Lee, A. E. Matthews, Donald Calthorp, Lillah McCarthy, Michael Sherbrook, Norman Page, Percy Marmont, Sydney Fairbrother, Norman McKinnel, A. E. George, Louis Calvert, Nigel Playfair, Graham Browne, C. V. France, J. D. Beveridge, George Tully, William Farren, junior, Dennis Eadie, J. H. Barnes, Florence Haydon, Frederick Lloyd, James Carew, Mabel Hackney, O. B. Clarence, Clare Greet, Madge McIntosh, Fanny Brough, Trever Lowe, Edmund Gurney, Henry Ainley, Edyth Olive, Eric Lewis, R. H. Hignett, Mrs. Patrick Campbell, Lawrence Irving, Holman Clark, and last and greatest, Ellen Terry.

There was in Granville Barker's producing a quality of imagination which impelled co-operation from the stage in a way that I have rarely seen equalled, and which to me is very reminiscent of the methods of Nikisch with his orchestra. So far as Barker was concerned every soul behind the footlights, from the leading lady to the lowest-paid scene-shifter, was automatically bound in a brotherhood of art; that any member of his staff, in any capacity whatever, was not all out for

absolute perfection never so much as entered his
head. And because he expected so much and put
so much of himself into his own work, he succeeded
in bringing out the best from everybody else.

One of his peculiarities, and one which was curiously effective, was that he would direct rehearsals
exactly as he would have conducted an orchestra.

" I want a tremendous *crescendo* here," he would
cry. " A sudden stop. *A firmata.* Now—down to
pianissimo ! "

Or, again :

" But, my dear child," he would lament, " you
deliver your lines as if you were the trombone,
whereas you really are the oboe in this *ensemble.*
Remember that, please. The oboe, *not* the trombone ! "

He was concerned, always—a quality which
naturally appealed very much to myself—that
the music should be on the same artistic level as
the plays he produced and the actors who performed
in them.

" Educate audiences," he was in the habit of
saying, " to come to the theatre with the idea that
music is one of the things they have paid money
to hear."

The enthusiasm of everybody concerned for
the musical programme was such, indeed, that in
order to be at hand for rehearsals at any odd hour,
I found it necessary to move nearer to the theatre.
When, however, it became the habit to haul me
out of bed in the small hours as if I were a general
practitioner urgently required for a dangerous

case, it occurred to me that it would be no bad idea to move back again to Regent's Park.

During these years at the Court it was inevitable that I should be brought into somewhat close personal association with Bernard Shaw, for during the Vedrenne-Barker reign no less than eleven of his plays were produced there: "Candida," "John Bull's Other Island," "How He Lied to Her Husband," "You Never Can Tell," "Man and Superman," "Major Barbara," "Captain Brassbound's Conversion," "The Doctor's Dilemma," "The Philanderer," "Don Juan in Hell," and "A Man of Destiny."

In consequence of these productions Shaw was constantly about the theatre. A more charming and sympathetic personality, nor, in his private capacity, one more wholly misrepresented, it would be difficult to encounter. And always in his dealings with everyone about the place was evident that strata of ironic humour which rendered association with him such sheer joy.

I remember, in particular, when Granville Barker was producing Gilbert Murray's version of Euripides' "Elektra" I was asked to compose suitable music for the Greek Chorus, a task more easily said than done.

The work had been in other hands before it came into mine, but with a sublime disregard for the limitations of ancient musical expression and the fact that in those times music as we know it did not exist, the composer had iconoclastically written the score for an eight-part chorus and modern instruments. In addition to these urgent difficulties there were but five days in which to complete the work.

Under these limitations, then, the task was accomplished at last by a committee of three, seated side by side upon the piano bench : Gilbert Murray, Granville Barker, and myself, each phrase as I played it being subjected to the close analysis of the other two, and accepted, rejected, or modified according to the joint decision. It was while we were over neck and ears in this concentrated work that word came Mr. Shaw would like to speak to Mr. Barker, to which the latter replied that as things were at the moment he was not going to leave the piano for Bernard Shaw or anybody else. Hence, as the mountain refused to go to Mahomet, there was no alternative but for Mahomet, in the person of Mr. Shaw, to come to the mountain. The door burst open and in Shaw came. He glanced at the three concentrated about the piano.

" Sheer waste, expending time and energy on all this rubbish," he pronounced.

Gilbert Murray, who, as already I have said, was responsible for the version of the play, looked up.

" What d'you mean, rubbish ? " he protested indignantly. To which the reply came from Shaw in silvery, soothing tones, and a suggestion of reproof that he could so have been misjudged :

" Not you, Murray ; I meant Euripides ! "

Another characteristic story of Shaw is connected with a girl who was one of the Chorus in this very production of Euripides, one who was as keen on her work as her position in the company was humble, and who approached me afterwards with a request that I should give her introductions to other conductors.

After Euripides was taken off I lost sight of her. Then, two years later, I received a printed invitation for a Dinner Party and At Home from a hostess who was absolutely unknown to me, even by name. In the course of conversation I happened to show the invitation to Taylor Platt, asking him casually if he happened to have any knowledge of the people who sent it.

" Yes," he said, " it's from a girl who was one of the Chorus in ' Elektra.' "

More out of curiosity than any other motive I accepted the invitation. When I reached the house, which was a large one in a fashionable neighbourhood, it was to find a very extreme contrast from the comparative poverty of the former Chorus girl and the obvious wealth of the great lady who was my hostess.

Chatting with her after dinner she was good enough to tell me her story. It appeared that she was the daughter of very wealthy people in Birmingham ; but that, as is not altogether unusual in such an environment, her parents had less sympathy with art than was quite compatible to their daughter. And so it was that after a series of somewhat violent scenes the girl had made her own bid for artistic expression by cutting the parental painter, and coming to London.

At the time when at long last she had been given a job in the "Elektra" Chorus, she was quite penniless, and as soon as that engagement was finished looked like being so again. It was then that, following her request to me, she had written to Bernard Shaw and asked him to grant her an interview, which with characteristic good-nature he had consented to. In the subsequent conversation she had had the good sense frankly to lay her cards on the table, inform him of her exact position, and ask for his advice as to what, under the circumstances, would be the best for her to do.

Shaw listened sympathetically, and the position assimilated, proceeded to tender counsel culled from his own philosophy and exact knowledge of life.

"This life will not bring you happiness," he pronounced. "If you wish to fulfil your nature you must go home and—have a baby."

So, in accordance with this disinterested counsel, the girl went home, and, having fallen in love with and married the English Consul in a Continental city, proceeded to fulfil her nature as Shaw had suggested.

It is eloquent of the standard achieved during the thirty-two months when Vedrenne and Barker ruled the destinies of the Court Theatre, that besides Shaw, amongst the seventeen dramatists produced there were included Laurence Housman, John Galsworthy, Henrik Ibsen, Maurice Hewlett, G. Hauptmann, W. B. Yeats, A. Schnitzler, John Masefield, and Maurice Maeterlinck.

When he was producing " Captain Brassbound's Conversion " it occurred to Barker that it would lend verisimilitude to the castle scene in the second act, where, it will be remembered, Lady Cecily and her party are imprisoned by Captain Brassbound and his following of renegade British sailors, if a chorus of English sea chanties was introduced. The difficulty, however, was to obtain the sea chanties, and he asked me to look some up in the British Museum library.

I suppose there *are* people with minds sufficiently trained to enable them to run any specific volume to earth in that vast acreage of massed literature, but I confess frankly that this was one of the few times in my life I have been obliged to admit failure in carrying out a job of work. Fortunately, I found Barker sympathetic.

" Don't worry," he said kindly. " As a matter of fact it doesn't matter a bit."

" How's that ? " I enquired. " Why doesn't it matter ? "

" Because by a curious coincidence I think it very likely we shall be able to get the chanties elsewhere," he said. " A boy came into my office to-day who's a deck hand on a wind-jammer trading to South America. In his spare time he makes a hobby of composing sea songs, and the words seem just about what we want."

" How about the music ? " I enquired.

" I think that will be all right too," Barker said. " He's made up some tunes as well. He doesn't know a note of music himself—he only whistles.

Anyway, I told him to come up to your office at eleven in the morning, and you can let me know what you think."

And sure enough at the appointed time on the following day a slim, poorly dressed, and very shy young seaman insinuated himself through the door of my sanctum.

" Mr. Barker told me to come and whistle to you," he said diffidently, twirling his cap in his hands.

" That's all right," I said. " Sit down and let me hear those sea chanties I've heard so much about."

So very stiff and upright in a chair, the young sailor went through the tunes that in his spare time he had composed in the forecastle of a wooden sailing ship.

When he got up to go, obviously relieved that his ordeal was at an end, I asked him his name.

" John Masefield," he said.

It was only a few months later that that same John Masefield's first play, " The Campden Wonder," was produced, in the same bill as Cyril Harcourt's " The Reformer," at the Court Theatre.

CHAPTER XVII

AS I have hinted already, Granville Barker was particularly insistent that the minor parts should be played with the same finish as was expected from the principal characters. As much as anything it is to this that the success of his regime was due. Indeed, it is not too much to write that so far as the Court Theatre was concerned there were not, in actual practice, any star performers, a claim which is illustrated by quoting an instance when, after making something of a sensation by his brilliant interpretation of " Straker " in Shaw's " Man and Superman," Edmund Gwenn was perfectly happy to make his next appearance in the quite minor part of Baines the butler in St. John Hankin's " Return of the Prodigal." As an example of the sincerity he brought to bear in the interpretation of a character who appears only for a very few moments, and with only a few words of dialogue which are not in the least crucial to the development of the plot, it is only necessary to mention that even with Mr. A. E. Matthews as the only other actor on the stage, for the brief space of his appearance Mr. Gwenn was the centre of interest.

I remember John Galsworthy paying a very sincere tribute to this insistence upon the finished

perfection with which the minor parts at the Court
Theatre were played. At the end of the first
performance of his " The Silver Box " he made a
special point of going behind the scenes to congratulate four of the supers for the work they had
put into the crowd scene. The names of that
quartette of minor parts, incidentally, were respec-
tively : Allan Wade, Norman Page, Lewis Casson,
and Edmund Gwenn.

Nor did it take Barker long to realise a fact,
which even now many producers are apt to over-
look, that while finished acting is able to lend
realism to inadequate scenery, even the most
elaborate stage setting can contribute nothing of
conviction to an indifferent performance. At the
Court Theatre, although there was little money to
spare for elaborate stage effects, it is certain that
any economies necessary in this direction were more
than compensated for by the strength and sincerity
of the acting, and also, be it said, by a certain
genius in utilising whatever material was at hand
in suggesting exactly the right atmosphere.

Apart from his stage work, as I knew him at
the Court Theatre Edmund Gwenn was of the
type who put earnestness and vitality into every
little action of the common day. Anything over
which one could afford to slack was simply not
worth doing. He was intensely athletic, and as
physically fit as fresh air and exercise could make
him ; a keen Rugger player, and rather more than
a useful boxer—so much so, in fact, that it has
since struck me that his personal dresser must

have been a man of robust constitution and somewhat varied gifts.

The intervals of Gwenn's appearance as Drink-
water in " Captain Brassbound's Conversion " used
to be employed in strenuous boxing bouts between
the pair, a practice which continued nightly until,
in the middle of one rather more than usually
vigorous set-to, the actor put his foot clean through
the floor of his dressing-room—which happened to
be the ceiling of Vedrenne's office.

Some idea of Gwenn's quality is indicated by
the circumstance that on the night which sealed
his reputation as an actor he was called upon to go
through his part under very considerable disability.

The play was Shaw's " Man and Superman," in
which as already I have mentioned he played
Henry Straker.

In the scene when Granville Barker, who played
John Tanner, was pulling him from under the car,
Gwenn caught his mouth on a spanner with sufficient force to knock a tooth clean out. But though
he must have been badly hampered in his articula-
tion and suffering a quite considerable amount of
pain, there was not a single person in the audience
with the slightest idea that anything untoward had
occurred. And that was the night, as I have said,
that Gwenn made his name.

Nor was this the only occasion Gwenn played his
part under physical handicap. In Elizabeth Robin's
play, " Votes for Women," without any warning
whatever his nose began to bleed profusely at the

AN ITALIAN IDYLL

very moment he received his cue to deliver one of
the longest speeches of the play.

Fortunately the other players in the scene very
quickly realised the situation. There must, they
felt, be some authenticity for the *contretemps*, so
with a flash of inspiration, and in order to provide
that verisimilitude Lowe, who was standing next
to him, pretended, deliberately, to hit him on the
nose. After that it was only in the natural order
that during the remainder of the speech Gwenn
should be handed relays of handkerchiefs to staunch
the flow resulting from the punishment which
ostensibly he had received. Even then, by the
time it came for him to make his exit, the moustache
of that black-haired actor was stained a ghastly
crimson.

But after all, the play's the thing, besides which
nothing counts or matters, and the success of that
loyal subterfuge may be gathered from a scrap
of conversation overheard between two ladies as
the audience was leaving the theatre after the fall
of the final curtain.

" It is perfectly astounding," one remarked to
the other, " the amount of realism that is brought
to bear at the Court ! "

Instantly to be able to grasp a situation, and
having grasped it, adequately to cope with it, is
one of the hall-marks of the finished actor. Granville Barker had this capacity very highly developed
indeed. When he was playing Valentine to Norman
Page's Philip Clandon in Shaw's " You Never Can
Tell," at the beginning of a section of very

tense dialogue, the latter completely lost his voice.

With an actor of less experience than Barker the mishap would have been fatal to the action of the play. Actually, however, there were few in the audience who realised what had occurred. For when it came to Philip Clandon's turn to speak, exactly as if it were part of the business, Barker would pretend to break in with an interruption, and turning to whichever character Page should have addressed, would say : " I know what he's going to say. It is —— " ; or, " Phil thinks —— "; and go on with the speech Page should have delivered.

I tender my tribute to that as the most ingenious and successful piece of stage bluff I ever witnessed.

A stage device which was perhaps not quite so completely successful occurred in " Captain Brassbound's Conversion," which it will be remembered Shaw wrote expressly for Ellen Terry towards the close of that great genius's wonderful stage career, and when her memory for the script was perhaps just a little hazy.

As counter to this peculiarity Miss Terry very ingeniously used to stick up postcards in the wings, upon which her part was written.

On one occasion, however, she most unfortunately stuck up all the cards for Act Four on the wings which should have been devoted to Act Two, with the somewhat disconcerting result that she made all her last act speeches, including the *dénouement*, in the second act, and left it for the audience and her fellow-actors to puzzle out what she was talking about.

There is a story in connection with this bad memory of Ellen Terry's which, since, I have heard fathered on to my friend, Sybil Thorndike, and whom I am quite sure would be the first to repudiate it. Actually the incident occurred when Bernard Shaw and Vedrenne were standing in the wings watching a rehearsal of " Captain Brass-bound's Conversion." Vedrenne listened to Ellen Terry for some little time with a rather puzzled expression on his face. Then he turned to Shaw.

" Is Miss Terry speaking the lines as you wrote them ? " he enquired.

Shaw shook his head.

" No," he said, " but she's speaking the lines as I ought to have written them."

At the fall of the curtain on the first night of " Candida " the house clamoured for a speech from Shaw, who did not appear. In order to quell the tumult Vedrenne walked on to the stage.

" I am not Shaw," he announced, " but probably you will find him on the platform of the station next door."

That speech was never finished, for with one accord the audience rose and left the theatre, presumably to induce Mr. Shaw to give them a short address from the platform of the Sloane Square Underground Station

But not always were audiences so appreciative. During the run of " Man and Superman " Granville Barker was unable to play owing to illness, and as was only fair, the box-office manager warned each purchaser of a ticket that the part of John Tanner would be played by a substitute. One gentleman assimilated the information in silence for a moment, debating, evidently, whether it would be wise to risk his money.

" It isn't Vedrenne who's playing, is it ? " he enquired at last.

" No, sir," came the reply. " Mr. Vedrenne isn't an actor."

The man sighed his relief.

" Thank God ! " he said, and thrust out the money. " Here, give me a ticket."

Before the performance of " The Doctor's Dilemma," which was a matinée on an extraordinarily hot day, the queues contained far more people than the house had accommodation for. In order to save disappointment Granville Barker sent warning to those in the rear of the waiting ranks that there was no chance of their admittance, and all but one of those so warned melted disconsolately away. This grim optimist, however, only moved up to join with those who remained.

" Somebody's bound to faint, in this weather," he exclaimed hopefully, " and then I can have the seat."

And sure enough someone did faint, and he had his reward.

At a command performance of " John Bull's Other Island," Vedrenne hired a special suite of furniture for the Royal box. And when the night came King Edward's laugh could be heard all over the house. As a matter of fact he laughed so heartily that he broke the chair that had been so especially provided for him ! And what is more Maples' sent in a bill for the damage !

Already mention has been made of John Galsworthy's play, " The Silver Box." It was rather curious how this play came to be accepted. It is not often, I think, that a dramatist sees one of his plays produced only because a previous effort has been destroyed. Vedrenne, however, told me that when " The Silver Box " was first discussed, he asked Galsworthy if he had written any other play.

" One," replied Galsworthy.

" What happened to it ? " enquired Vedrenne.

" I burnt it," said Galsworthy.

" That decided me," Vedrenne told me. " There's always hope for people who burn their plays."

I wonder if there is hope, also, for people who discard their more material sustenance. What gives rise to the thought is a very vivid recollection of how Lewis Casson and I got rid of an unwanted meal.

We were standing outside the theatre one noon, when very diffidently and politely we were approached by a very charming, but, I imagine, not too affluent middle-aged lady.

" Pardon me," she said courteously, " but am I correct in assuming that you are from the theatre ? "

We admitted that such, indeed, was the case.

" My sister and I," the lady continued, " have started a little restaurant almost next door, where we provide only home-cooked meals, and at a very reasonable price. If only we can obtain the people from the theatre as customers, it would mean so very much to us. I wonder, then, if you will consent to lunch there to-day. We will do everything we can to give you a really nice meal, so that if you are satisfied you can recommend us to your friends at the theatre."

As such a place as she described was exactly what everybody connected with the theatre had for a long time been wanting, both Lewis and myself very gladly welcomed the opportunity.

But alas, clean and wholesome as the small premises were, the food provided proved to be absolutely hopeless. Our order was the quite unambitious one of roast beef and potatoes. The meat was a thick slab of some raw red substance which only the ladies' manifest sincerity enabled us to accept as beef; the potatoes were solid balls of putty-like soapiness.

Everything was entirely uneatable. But what to do about it ? The last thing possible was to hurt the feelings of those two poor women by leaving the food on our plates. To eat it was equally impossible.

So, leaving the amount of our bill on the table, and smuggling the revolting mess into our handkerchiefs, with the air of conspirators we stole softfooted from the restaurant.

Only those who have sought to dispose of unwanted substance in the busy streets of London will be able to realise our dilemma. For the next half-hour the eyes of the whole metropolis seemed fixed on us as inextricably and inexorably as if we were two great heroes, or, alternatively, even greater criminals. There did not seem to be one inch of London where, without observation, a man could leave a slab of raw beef. And in the meanwhile the red blood of that meat had saturated our handkerchiefs, and was penetrating deeply into the lining of our pockets even to the texture of the cloth which covered them.

" Once we take it out," Lewis Casson muttered in gloomy warning, " inevitably we shall be arrested for murder." Then his face registered a ray of hope. " Why not drown it ? " he suggested.

So with the gait and demeanour of two more than usually culpable homicides we sneaked furtively to Chelsea Embankment, where, summoning our theatrical training to our aid, we leaned over the parapet as though intent upon the scene that Whistler has immortalised.

And there, at long last, with the stealth of serpents and the sleight of hand of professional conjurers, we dropped our loathsome loads into the river.

It was the considered policy of the Court Theatre management that in the event of a complaint the patron was always in the right ; in other words they went out of their way to study the convenience, and if necessary the idiosyncrasies, of the audience.

Speaking generally, the policy was wise, and in the end, profitable. Nevertheless there were times when individual members of the public proved more than a little unreasonable. I remember Taylor Platt, the business manager, asking me into his office one afternoon to listen to a forthcoming telephone conversation. It appeared that a lady who, from one of the best addresses in the West End, had booked the most expensive box in the house for the previous night's performance, and to which she had driven in a most elaborate carriage and pair complete with liveried coachman and footman, had telephoned earlier in the day to report the loss of—half a shilling packet of chocolates, which she believed had been left in her box. Would Mr. Platt kindly cause enquiries to be made, ascertain if this had been found, and telephone her at four o'clock ? It was to the latter conversation I had been called in to listen. Incidentally I may mention that after every performance quite a number of half-consumed boxes of chocolates were retrieved from all parts of the house, and quite naturally regarded as the legitimate perquisities of the attendants.

Platt, however, with the utmost gravity obeyed the lady's injunction to report the result of the search for her sixpen'orth of sweets.

" I very much regret, Madam," he said courteously, " that after the most exhaustive search your chocolates cannot be traced. However, so that you may not be the loser, if you will honour me by calling at the theatre, I shall be glad for you to choose any box of chocolates from our stock."

And, unbelievable though it may read, the lady

duly arrived in her carriage and selected a shilling packet of chocolate from the dress circle bar.

With a theatre as popular as the Court at that time it was inevitable that we should have occasional encounters with individual members of the audience, and some of these were very amusing. Take, for instance, the gentleman who one night presented himself at the booking-office when quite obviously in a condition I understand is known as having partaken of " one over the eight," and who, very politely but firmly, the box-office attendant refused to pass into the theatre.

The gentleman looked very hurt at this.

" *Why* won't you sell me a seat ? " he demanded indignantly.

" Frankly, because you're not quite sober," explained the attendant.

From protest the applicant's attitude changed to one of immense surprise.

" Do you mean I'm drunk ? " he questioned.

" Yes," said the attendant.

" But of *course* I'm drunk," the other explained. " Do you think I should come to the Court Theatre if I was sober ? "

The subject of drink reminds me that, besides being a non-smoker and vegetarian, Granville Barker was a very strict teetotaller. Only once did I ever know him depart from that rule, and even then it was by way of being involuntarily. In Ibsen's " The Wild Duck " is a scene where Hialmar Ekdal, whom he impersonated, is required to drink a glass of beer.

The property man was instructed always to provide a harmless substitute for this, but upon one occasion omitted to do so, so that it was the real article Barker was called upon to consume, and owing to his rigidly abstemious habits, with quite obvious results.

This carries my mind automatically to food consumed upon the stage. The luncheon that was served in " You Never Can Tell " was a very real and substantial meal, and was sent in each night piping hot from the Queen's Restaurant near-by. I remember that Edmund Gurney, who played Fergus Crampton, insisted always upon being served with a generous helping of chicken—we used to accuse him of going without lunch for the run of that particular play !

One night this demand of Gurney's was taken advantage of by Norman Page to turn into a really excellent practical joke. He procured a hare's foot from the dressing-room of one of the girls, dressed and especially prepared it, and arranged with Percy Marmont, who played the waiter, that it should be served to Gurney, whose chagrin when he attempted to stick his fork into it, and it shot clear across the table to find resting-place directly in the astonished face of Lillah McCarthy, was a revelation of the possibilities of human expression.

As a matter of fact we were all so friendly at the Court Theatre that practical jokes were common, usually with Norman Page, who shared a dressing-room with Edmund Gwenn, as conspirator-in-chief.

At that time Gurney used invariably to dress in a frock-coat and tall hat, and, even in the height of summer, insisted always upon carrying an old-fashioned and not too meticulously rolled umbrella, into the interior of which upon one occasion Norman Page inserted a generous supply of small green apples.

Nothing happened for a day or two, so that we were under the impression that having discovered the trick the prospective victim had removed the fruit and decided that the best counter to it lay in silence. What we had omitted to take into account, however, was that just then the weather had been unusually fine, and thus the use of an umbrella had been unnecessary. On the evening of the first wet day, however, Gurney burst into Norman Page's dressing-room, and with a wealth of imagery that was a tribute as much to the vividness of his imagination as to his vocabulary, let it be known that the plot had succeeded.

" It was in Oxford Street this afternoon," he said in his sonorous voice, " that I met a lady of my acquaintance—and a very charming lady too, let me tell you. Well, it came on to rain, and, of course, I offered her the use of my umbrella." He paused impressively. " And when I came to open it over her head," he announced dramatically at last, " out fell a ruddy orchard ! "

I was in Platt's office one day when my eyes happened to fall upon a very ornate but, by then, rather dusty opera hat, which for quite a long time had been hanging on one of the pegs. I remarked chaffingly about it, and he told me its history.

Months previously a man in evening dress, accompanied by two ladies, in taking his seat in the stalls, which was next to the side gangway, hung his hat on an electric light bracket on the wall. As this was strictly against the rule of the house, one of the girl attendants had asked him, very politely, to remove it. This the man refused to do, so the girl had no alternative but to call a man attendant to deal with him, but with a similar lack of result.

As the responsibility for carrying out the regulations was his, very rightly the man had reported the matter to Platt.

Platt left his office, and went into the stalls, where as courteously as possible he asked the man to remove his hat.

" It is not so much that it is against our rules for it to be there," he explained, " as that it is directly contrary to the regulations of the London County Council. I'm perfectly willing for the attendant to take your hat to the cloakroom, and to bring you the ticket here. But in any case I must ask you to remove your hat from the bracket."

Whether it was that having once taken a stand the man was too pig-headed to climb down, or whether he merely wished to impress his lady companions with his firmness, is unknown. In any case, and to Platt's surprise and annoyance, the man still resolutely declined to relinquish the unreasonable position he had taken up.

Thus Platt had no alternative but to resort to other measures.

" Very well," he said, " I shall take your hat into my office, and if you want it you will have to come and get it."

" And there," Platt said, with a gesture towards the peg upon which it hung, " it remains still."

Upon another occasion Platt was in his office when the box-office attendant reported that one of the audience had demanded his money back, so far as he could understand, for no apparent reason, and that he insisted upon seeing Platt personally. As it was the considered policy of the theatre to investigate every complaint to the full, Platt had the man shown up, who proved to be a rather well-dressed middle-aged gentleman of somewhat excitable appearance.

" I understand you have asked for the return of your money," Platt said. " May I ask what is your complaint ? "

" I have nothing at all to say against the performance," said his visitor. " My complaint is that I can't get anything fit to eat here."

" But, my dear sir," Platt protested, " this is a theatre, not a restaurant."

" Nevertheless, I've come here straight from the City," the man argued, " and naturally I want something to eat."

The point of view was so unusual that for a moment it left Platt rather nonplussed.

" What about a bar or so of chocolate to keep you going until supper ? " he said.

" Because," said his visitor, " I only eat So-and-so's chocolate, and that you don't sell here."

" Then why not go into the bar," prompted Platt, anxious to find a way out, " and have a few biscuits ? "—a suggestion which only appeared to add fuel to the fire.

" Am I a dog that I should live on biscuits ? " the man demanded haughtily.

Platt glanced at his watch.

" Look here," he said patiently. " There's an interval of a quarter of an hour in a few minutes—ample time for you to slip across to the Queen's Restaurant, have a bite of food and be back before the curtain goes up for the next act. Why not do that ? "

" Because," said the man, " I have no desire to leave the theatre."

Well, there it was. Nothing Platt could say was able to convince his patron that he had not a legitimate cause for grievance ; that, as well as a theatrical entertainment, it was not a gross breach of contract between management and public that the Court Theatre was unable to supply a table d'hôte dinner.

Eventually Platt had no alternative but, declining further discussion, to show his aggrieved patron the door.

In a volume of theatrical reminiscences I read recently I was amazed to find the author referring to Mrs. Patrick Campbell as being universally unpopular. I use the word " amazed " advisedly, because at the time she played Hedda Tesman in

Ibsen's " Hedda Gabler " at the Court that was very far indeed from being the case.

I think perhaps it may be that her strong personality and very pronounced views are the cause of her having made enemies ; equally I am certain that those same qualities, allied to a natural charm of manner, have earned her the lasting love and respect of many people who really matter.

An instance of her individuality of view occurred during the very engagement I have just mentioned. I had chosen as the item to be played during one of the intervals a gavotte by Bach. As soon as it was over I was approached by the call boy.

" Mrs. Pat's compliments, and she would like to know the name of that awful twiddly music the orchestra have just been playing," he said.

However, I had the satisfaction of pointing out to her later, that a man who had occupied the same seat for the whole seven performances had slept solidly through the whole of the four acts, including the time when she herself was on the stage, only to come to life to listen intently to the orchestral selections during the interval.

I have never ceased to regard Granville Barker's retirement from producing as a great calamity for British dramatic art. He was only twenty-seven when with Vedrenne he took over the reins at the Court Theatre, and in those two-and-a-half years his natural genius for production became reinforced with an experience which could not fail to have brought him an influence in the world of the theatre greater, even, than already he had come to possess.

When he was producing Bernard Shaw's " Androcles and the Lion " in America, I introduced him to Pavlova in my lodgings in New York, and in the conversation which followed she conceived a great admiration for his artistic ideals.

Later, when she consulted me as to the production of a new ballet and I suggested his " Prunelle," her thoughts flew instantly to the author. She asked me to get into touch with him as to the rights of the performance, and, if an arrangement could be come to, if he could see his way to let her have the benefit of his suggestions and advice. Hence I wrote to him, and said that I very much wished to see him to discuss a subject of great artistic importance. In due time a reply came— a cordial friendly letter, in which he said how glad he was to hear of me again. But to any possible suggestion of a return to his old activity, he was utterly unresponsive.

" If you want," he wrote, " to talk to me about the theatre, don't ; for I've done with the theatre for ever and a day."

And that is one of the saddest letters I ever received.

CHAPTER XVIII

STRICTLY speaking, I suppose that in a book designed to deal with my association with Madame Pavlova, of the adventures which befell us over that three hundred thousand miles of travel throughout the habitable globe, and to convey some idea of a striking and fascinating personality, the three preceding chapters should have no part.

If such is necessary, my apology for their inclusion is that it was in the years I was attached to the Drawing-room Orchestra that played at Sandringham, and perhaps more particularly during the period I was wholly responsible for the musical programme at the Court Theatre, that I gained the peculiar experience which enabled me to fulfil the requirements it is so necessary for the Musical Director for the Pavlova Company to possess.

Nevertheless it was not until after considerable doubt I decided to include those three chapters.

I was led to do so at last by the representations of friends with whom I discussed the form and available material of the book before I came to compile it.

They pointed out, and I am inclined to think with reason, that it would be no ill compliment to Pavlova to include in a book of which she was the inspiration some brief account of my association with other figures whose names and achievements are written beside her own in the scroll of artistic endeavour. Indeed, in a review of my own career, it seems to me now that those years before I joined the Pavlova Company were a time of preparation for the exacting, but wholly absorbing, era that was to come. I feel that sixteen years to have been the culmination of my life work.

In that time Pavlova has been one of the greatest missionaries for culture of her time, for she has spread the light of her genius into the dark places of the world ; taken her company into areas where hitherto such undertaking had been impracticable, and before peoples thought to be impervious to artistic influence. And in the campaign it was my privilege to be her lieutenant and coadjutant. And to have been that is to have had no small honour.

It is a reflection as true as it is sad that, however close and mutually satisfying, sooner or later every human association must have its end. The end of my Musical Directorship for Anna Pavlova came after sixteen years.

In that severance it is a source of consolation and happiness that our friendship remains yet firm and unbroken. I think I may say that the parting of the ways came through no wish either of my own or of hers. It came because I was physically incapable of withstanding the strain any longer.

In that period I had travelled a distance which

represents over ten times the circumference of the
world, and for weeks together stayed in no one
city for more than twenty-four hours. Apart from
the not inconsiderable work and anxiety entailed
by the continual rehearsing of strange and, more
often than not, incompetent orchestras ; of arranging and rearranging scores ; and of selecting and
composing music for new productions, the actual
physical and nervous strain of conducting had
made serious inroads into my vitality. I had
received a warning which no longer could be
denied. Mentally and physically I was a tired man.

It was only in the natural course of things that
it was to M. Dandré I first tendered my resignation,
for it is he who deals with the interior administration of the company. It lay with him to break
the news to Madame. Thus by the time I saw her
she also had come to realise that the parting of the
ways had come.

The last time I conducted for her was at her own
farewell performance to London for the Season
which ended on Saturday, October 24th, 1925.

To me that was an unforgettable occasion, and
one which in its sadness I should not care to have
repeated. That night Pavlova, M. Dandré, the
Company, and my own loyal comrades of the
Orchestra vied with each other in showing me,
by every means their own kind hearts could suggest
or goodwill and friendship devise, that the parting
from their " Maestro " was to them a matter of
affectionate regret.

After I had laid down my baton as Pavlova's

conductor for the last time, I was called up beside her on the stage, there to be presented with mementoes both from the company and from the Orchestra. That, without knowing, both had chosen identical presents does not detract from the poignantly grateful value I place upon those concrete expressions of their regard.

And at the last Pavlova walked off the stage, leaving to me the honour of taking that last farewell from the audience whom so many times over the years it had been our mutual privilege to serve.

There is an occasion in the future, however, and long delayed though I hope that occasion may be, when it will be my melancholy pride once more to take up my baton to conduct for Madame Anna Pavlova. That will be at her own farewell performance. Wherever in the world that good-bye takes place, it will be a combination of very adverse circumstances which will prevent me from paying that last tribute to the greatest artist and the greatest woman I have ever met.

And as a farewell to my readers, now, I can find no more fitting term than the words with which Sir Henry Irving was accustomed to bid good-bye to his audience :

I am your most grateful and obedient servant,

THEODORE STIER.

THE END

Lightning Source UK Ltd.
Milton Keynes UK
UKHW040708250820
368797UK00004B/1331